JavaScript Study Companion

Learn, Practice, and Apply JavaScript Fundamentals

By Laurence Lars Svekis

Dedicated to

Alexis and Sebastian

Thank you for your support

For more content and to learn more, visit

https://basescripts.com/

Introduction

Overview of What You'll Learn

This book is designed to provide you with a solid foundation in JavaScript, the language that powers modern web development. Whether you're looking to enhance your coding skills, kickstart a career in tech, or simply explore the exciting world of programming, this book equips you with the essential knowledge and hands-on experience to succeed. You will learn:

- **JavaScript Basics**: Understand variables, data types, operators, and syntax.
- **Control Flow**: Master if/else statements, loops, and switch cases for decision-making in your code.
- **Functions and Scope**: Learn how to create reusable code and manage variables effectively.
- **DOM Manipulation**: Explore how JavaScript interacts with web pages to create dynamic, interactive content.

- **Error Handling**: Gain confidence in identifying and resolving coding errors.
- **Advanced Topics**: Delve into arrays, objects, and event handling to build functional and efficient applications.

By the end of this book, you'll not only understand the "what" and "why" behind JavaScript concepts but also confidently apply them to solve real-world problems.

Who This Book Is For

This book is perfect for:

- **Complete Beginners**: If you've never written a line of code before, this book will guide you step-by-step.
- **Aspiring Web Developers**: If you want to build websites or web applications, this book lays the groundwork for JavaScript proficiency.
- **Students and Enthusiasts**: Whether you're studying programming or exploring coding as a hobby, this book offers an accessible and practical approach.

Target Audience

- **Complete Beginners**: No prior coding knowledge is required.
- **Aspiring Developers**: This book helps you prepare for more advanced programming topics.
- **Self-Learners**: If you enjoy learning at your own pace, this book is structured to support independent study.

Prerequisites

- **Basic Computer Literacy**: Familiarity with using a computer, a web browser, and text editing software.
- **Curiosity and Motivation**: A desire to learn, experiment, and problem-solve will take you far.

How to Use This Book

This book is structured to take you on a journey from understanding JavaScript fundamentals to applying them in practical scenarios. Here's how to make the most of it:

1. Structure and Progression of the Content

- The book begins with **fundamental concepts** such as variables and syntax, building a strong base for deeper topics.
- Each chapter builds on the previous one, introducing **incremental challenges** to reinforce learning.
- Exercises, quizzes, and examples help you apply your knowledge to **real-world scenarios**.
- Advanced chapters prepare you for **complex JavaScript topics** like DOM manipulation and event handling.

2. Tips for Effective Learning and Practice

- **Read Actively**: Take notes, highlight important sections, and ask questions as you read.
- **Practice Frequently**: Complete the exercises at the end of each chapter. Repetition is key to mastering coding concepts.
- **Experiment**: Modify the code examples provided in the book and observe how changes affect the results.

- **Seek Help**: Use online forums or programming communities if you encounter challenges.
- **Be Patient**: Learning to code takes time. Celebrate small wins along the way.

By following these tips and engaging with the material, you'll develop the skills and confidence needed to write JavaScript code effectively.

JavaScript Basics

JavaScript is a versatile programming language primarily used for web development. It allows developers to add interactivity to websites and create dynamic web applications. This introductory content focuses on JavaScript's basic syntax and structure, covering topics necessary to answer the quiz questions below.

1. Comments in JavaScript

Comments help you explain your code and make it more readable. JavaScript supports two types of comments:

Single-line comments: Use //.

```
// This is a single-line comment
let x = 5; // Assign 5 to x
```

Multi-line comments: Use /* ... */.

```
/* This is a multi-line comment
   that spans multiple lines */
let y = 10;
```

2. Declaring Variables

Variables store data for later use. JavaScript provides three ways to declare variables:

- **var**: Older way to declare variables.
- **let**: Modern way; block-scoped.
- **const**: For values that should not be reassigned.

Example:

```
var name = "John";
let age = 30;
const country = "USA";
```

3. Data Types

JavaScript supports several data types:

String: Text enclosed in quotes.
```
let greeting = "Hello, World!";
```

Number: Numeric values (integers or floats).
```
let score = 95;
```

Boolean: True or false values.
```
let isLoggedIn = true;
```

Undefined: Variable declared but not assigned.
```
let unknown;
```

Null: Represents "nothing".
```
let empty = null;
```

4. Operators

Operators perform operations on variables and values:

Arithmetic operators: +, -, *, /, % (modulus)

```
let sum = 5 + 10; // 15
```

Comparison operators: ==, ===, !=, <, >
```
let isEqual = (5 === "5"); // false
```

Logical operators: &&, ||, !
```
let isEligible = (age > 18 && hasLicense);
```

5. Writing Code Statements

JavaScript statements end with a semicolon (;). Multiple statements can be written on separate lines or combined on a single line:

```
let x = 10;
```

```
let y = 20; let sum = x + y;
```

6. Strings and String Concatenation

Strings can be combined using the + operator:

```
let firstName = "Jane";
let lastName = "Doe";
let fullName = firstName + " " + lastName;
// "Jane Doe"
```

You can also embed expressions using **template literals** (backticks ` `):

```
let message = `Hello, ${firstName}!`;
```

7. Writing Functions

Functions are reusable blocks of code:

```
function greet(name) {
   return `Hello, ${name}!`;
}
console.log(greet("Alice")); // "Hello, Alice!"
```

8. Conditionals

Use if, else if, and else to control program flow:

```
let age = 20;
if (age >= 18) {
  console.log("Adult");
} else {
  console.log("Minor");
}
```

Multiple-Choice Questions

What symbol is used for single-line comments in JavaScript?

1. /*
2. //
3. #
4. --

Answer: 2. //
Explanation: Single-line comments in JavaScript start with //. For multi-line comments, use /* ... */.

Which of the following declares a constant in JavaScript?

1. var
2. let
3. const
4. constant

Answer: 3. const
Explanation: const is used to declare variables whose values cannot be reassigned.

What will the following code output?

```
let x = 10;
let y = "10";
console.log(x === y);
```

1. true
2. false
3. undefined
4. NaN

Answer: 2. false
Explanation: The === operator checks both value and

type. Since x is a number and y is a string, the result is
`false`.

What is the correct way to write a string in JavaScript?
1. `"Hello"`
2. `'Hello'`
3. `` `Hello` ``
4. All of the above

Answer: 4. All of the above
Explanation: Strings in JavaScript can be enclosed in double quotes, single quotes, or backticks.

What will the following code output?
```
let sum = 5 + "5";
console.log(sum);
```
1. `10`
2. `"55"`
3. `undefined`
4. NaN

Answer: 2. `"55"`
Explanation: Adding a number and a string results in string concatenation.

What does the typeof operator return for let x;?
1. `"null"`
2. `"undefined"`
3. `"object"`
4. `"variable"`

Answer: 2. `"undefined"`
Explanation: A variable declared but not assigned has the type undefined.

What is the output of this code?

```
let a = true, b = false;
console.log(a || b);
```

    1. true

    2. false

    3. undefined

    4. null

Answer: 1. true

Explanation: The || operator returns true if either operand is true.

Which operator is used to check both value and type?

    1. =

    2. ==

    3. ===

    4. !==

Answer: 3. ===

Explanation: The === operator checks both value and type.

How do you declare a variable that can be reassigned?

    1. let

    2. const

    3. var

    4. Both 1 and 3

Answer: 4. Both 1 and 3

Explanation: Variables declared with let or var can be reassigned, but const cannot.

What is the result of the following code?

```
let a = 10;
let b = 20;
```

```
console.log(`${a + b}`);
```
    1. 1020

    2. 30

    3. "30"

    4. undefined

Answer: 3. "30"
Explanation: Template literals return strings, so the result is "30".

What is the correct syntax to define a function in JavaScript?

    1. `function myFunction {}`

    2. `function myFunction() {}`

    3. `def myFunction() {}`

    4. `function: myFunction() {}`

Answer: 2. `function myFunction() {}`
Explanation: Functions in JavaScript are defined using the `function` keyword followed by the function name and parentheses.

Which of the following is not a JavaScript data type?

    1. `String`

    2. `Number`

    3. `Float`

    4. `Boolean`

Answer: 3. `Float`
Explanation: JavaScript does not have a specific `Float` data type; all numbers, whether integers or floats, are of type `Number`.

What will the following code output?
```
let result = "5" - 3;
console.log(result);
```

1. 2
2. "53"
3. NaN
4. undefined

Answer: 1. 2
Explanation: The - operator converts the string "5" into a number, so the result is 2.

How do you declare a multi-line comment in JavaScript?
1. `<!-- Comment -->`
2. `// Comment //`
3. `/* Comment */`
4. `-- Comment --`

Answer: 3. `/* Comment */`
Explanation: Multi-line comments in JavaScript are enclosed in `/* ... */`.

Which operator is used to assign a value to a variable?
1. `=`
2. `==`
3. `===`
4. `=>`

Answer: 1. `=`
Explanation: The = operator is used to assign values to variables in JavaScript.

What will this code output?
```
console.log(typeof null);
```
1. `"null"`
2. `"undefined"`

3. `"object"`
4. `"number"`

Answer: 3. `"object"`
Explanation: This is a historical bug in JavaScript; `typeof null` returns `"object"`.

What does the console.log function do?
1. It displays output on the web page.
2. It logs a message to the browser's console.
3. It stores a log file on the server.
4. It sends a message to the user.

Answer: 2. It logs a message to the browser's console.
Explanation: The `console.log` function is used for debugging by displaying messages in the developer console.

What is the output of the following code?
```
let x;
console.log(x);
```
1. `undefined`
2. `null`
3. `NaN`
4. `0`

Answer: 1. `undefined`
Explanation: A declared variable without a value is `undefined`.

What is the result of this code?
```
let x = 5, y = "5";
console.log(x == y);
```
1. `true`
2. `false`
3. `undefined`

4. null

Answer: 1. `true`
Explanation: The `==` operator compares values but not types, so it evaluates as `true`.

Which keyword is used to declare a variable that cannot be reassigned?

1. `var`
2. `let`
3. `const`
4. `static`

Answer: 3. `const`
Explanation: Variables declared with `const` cannot be reassigned.

What does the following code output?
```
console.log(2 + "2");
```
1. `"22"`
2. 4
3. NaN
4. `undefined`

Answer: 1. `"22"`
Explanation: When adding a number and a string, JavaScript performs string concatenation.

Which of these is a correct variable name in JavaScript?

1. `2name`
2. `name-2`
3. `my_name`
4. `my name`

Answer: 3. my_name
Explanation: Variable names must not start with a number or contain spaces or special characters (other than _ or $).

What is the default value of an uninitialized variable in JavaScript?
1. 0
2. null
3. undefined
4. NaN

Answer: 3. undefined
Explanation: Uninitialized variables in JavaScript default to undefined.

What does the + operator do when used with strings?
1. Adds two numbers.
2. Performs string concatenation.
3. Converts strings to numbers.
4. Returns undefined.

Answer: 2. Performs string concatenation.
Explanation: The + operator concatenates strings, joining them together.

What will the following code output?
```
let greeting = "Hello";
let name = "Alice";
console.log(`${greeting}, ${name}!`);
```
1. Hello Alice!
2. Hello, Alice!
3. "Hello Alice!"
4. "Hello, Alice!"

Answer: 4. `"Hello, Alice!"`
Explanation: Template literals allow embedding variables and expressions, resulting in `"Hello, Alice!"`.

Variables and Data Types in JavaScript

1. Variables in JavaScript

Variables are used to store and manipulate data in JavaScript. There are three ways to declare variables:

- `var`: The traditional way to declare variables, with function scope.
- `let`: A modern way to declare variables, with block scope.
- `const`: For declaring variables that cannot be reassigned, with block scope.

Declaring Variables

Here's how you declare variables with `var`, `let`, and `const`:

```
var name = "John"; // Function-scoped
variable
let age = 30;      // Block-scoped variable
const country = "USA"; // Constant value
```

2. Rules for Naming Variables

- Variable names can include letters, numbers, _, and $.
- Names must not start with a number.
- Reserved keywords (e.g., `let`, `const`) cannot be used as names.

```
let userName = "Alice"; // Valid
let _score = 100;       // Valid
```

```
let 1stPlace = true;      // Invalid (starts
with a number)
```

3. Data Types in JavaScript

JavaScript is a dynamically typed language, meaning variables can hold any data type, which can change at runtime.

String: Text data enclosed in quotes.
```
let greeting = "Hello";
```

Number: Numeric data (integer or floating-point).
```
let age = 25;
```
```
let price = 19.99;
```

Boolean: Represents true or false.
```
let isLoggedIn = true;
```

Undefined: A variable declared but not assigned.
```
let unknown; // undefined
```

Null: Represents "nothing" or an empty value.
```
let empty = null;
```

Symbol: Represents unique identifiers.
```
let uniqueID = Symbol();
```

BigInt: For numbers beyond the safe integer limit.
```
let bigNumber =
12345678901234567890123456789012345678 90n;
```

Object: Used for complex data structures.
```
let user = { name: "John", age: 30 };
```

4. Key Differences Between var, let, and const

Feature	var	let	const

Scope	Function scope	Block scope	Block scope
Reassignment	Allowed	Allowed	Not allowed
Hoisting	Hoisted with `undefined`	Hoisted but not initialized	Hoisted but not initialized

Examples:

```
// var example
var name = "Alice";
name = "Bob"; // Allowed
// let example
let age = 25;
age = 30; // Allowed
// const example
const country = "Canada";
// country = "USA"; // Error: Assignment to
constant variable
```

Multiple-Choice Questions

Which keyword is used to declare a block-scoped variable?

1. var
2. let
3. const
4. Both 2 and 3

Answer: 4. Both 2 and 3
Explanation: Variables declared with let and const are block-scoped, meaning they are only accessible within the block where they are defined.

What is the default value of a variable declared but not assigned?

1. `null`
2. `undefined`
3. `0`
4. `false`

Answer: 2. `undefined`
Explanation: Variables in JavaScript are automatically assigned the value `undefined` if they are declared but not initialized.

What will this code output?

```
let a;
console.log(a);
```

1. `null`
2. `undefined`
3. `0`
4. NaN

Answer: 2. `undefined`
Explanation: The variable a is declared but not initialized, so its value is `undefined`.

Which keyword should be used for variables that will not change?

1. `var`
2. `let`
3. `const`
4. `immutable`

Answer: 3. `const`
Explanation: Variables declared with `const` cannot be reassigned.

What is the scope of a variable declared with var?

1. Block scope
2. Function scope
3. Global scope
4. Both 2 and 3

Answer: 4. Both 2 and 3
Explanation: var is function-scoped if declared inside a function; otherwise, it is globally scoped.

Which of the following is a primitive data type?

1. `Object`
2. `Array`
3. `Symbol`
4. `Function`

Answer: 3. Symbol
Explanation: Symbol is a primitive data type used for creating unique identifiers.

What will the following code output?

```
const x = 10;
x = 20;
console.log(x);
```

1. 10
2. 20
3. undefined
4. Error

Answer: 4. Error
Explanation: Reassigning a variable declared with const causes an error.

What does the following code output?

```
console.log(typeof null);
```

1. "null"

2. `"undefined"`
3. `"object"`
4. `"number"`

Answer: 3. `"object"`
Explanation: Due to a historical quirk in JavaScript, `null` is considered an object.

What is the result of this code?

```
var a = 5;
{
  var a = 10;
}
console.log(a);
```

1. 5
2. 10
3. undefined
4. Error

Answer: 2. 10
Explanation: Variables declared with `var` are not block-scoped, so the a inside the block overwrites the outer a.

What is the scope of a variable declared with let?

1. Block scope
2. Function scope
3. Global scope
4. Module scope

Answer: 1. Block scope
Explanation: Variables declared with `let` are only accessible within the block where they are defined.

Which of the following is true about const?

1. It cannot be reassigned.
2. It must be initialized when declared.

3. It is block-scoped.
4. All of the above

Answer: 4. All of the above
Explanation: const variables cannot be reassigned, must be initialized, and are block-scoped.

What is the data type of typeof NaN?
1. "number"
2. "NaN"
3. "undefined"
4. "string"

Answer: 1. "number"
Explanation: NaN is a special value in JavaScript of type number.

Which keyword is used for variables that can be reassigned within a block?
1. var
2. let
3. const
4. None of the above

Answer: 2. let
Explanation: Variables declared with let can be reassigned and are block-scoped.

Which of these is not a valid variable name?
1. _userName
2. $price
3. user-name
4. userName2

Answer: 3. user-name
Explanation: Hyphens (-) are not allowed in JavaScript variable names.

What will this code output?

```
let x = 10;
x += 5;
console.log(x);
```

    1. 10
    2. 15
    3. undefined
    4. Error

Answer: 2. 15

Explanation: The += operator adds 5 to the current value of x.

Let me know if you'd like the remaining questions or further assistance!

What happens when a var variable is redeclared in the same scope?

    1. It causes an error.
    2. It overrides the previous declaration.
    3. It is ignored.
    4. It creates a new variable.

Answer: 2. It overrides the previous declaration.

Explanation: Redeclaring a var variable in the same scope does not throw an error and simply overrides the previous value.

What will this code output?

```
let x = 5;
{
  let x = 10;
  console.log(x);
}
console.log(x);
```

    1. 5 and 10

2. 10 and 5
3. 10 and 10
4. Error

Answer: 2. 10 and 5
Explanation: The inner `let` x is block-scoped and does not affect the outer `let` x.

Which of the following can be used to declare variables?
1. `let`
2. `var`
3. `const`
4. All of the above

Answer: 4. All of the above
Explanation: JavaScript allows variables to be declared using `var`, `let`, or `const`.

What will the following code output?
```
const arr = [1, 2, 3];
arr.push(4);
console.log(arr);
```
1. `[1, 2, 3]`
2. `[1, 2, 3, 4]`
3. `Error`
4. `undefined`

Answer: 2. `[1, 2, 3, 4]`
Explanation: While `const` prevents reassignment of the variable `arr`, the contents of the array can still be modified.

Which of the following is not a valid JavaScript data type?
1. `String`
2. `Number`

3. Character
4. Boolean

Answer: 3. Character
Explanation: JavaScript does not have a Character data type. Strings represent text, including single characters.

What is the result of the following code?

```
let x = 10;
x = "Hello";
console.log(typeof x);
```

1. "number"
2. "string"
3. Error
4. "undefined"

Answer: 2. "string"
Explanation: JavaScript allows variables to change types, so x becomes a string.

What does let provide that var does not?

1. Block scope
2. Hoisting
3. Reassignment
4. None of the above

Answer: 1. Block scope
Explanation: let variables are block-scoped, unlike var, which is function-scoped.

What will this code output?

```
console.log(typeof undefined);
```

1. "null"
2. "object"
3. "undefined"
4. "string"

Answer: 3. `"undefined"`
Explanation: The `typeof` operator returns `"undefined"` for variables that are not initialized or explicitly set to `undefined`.

What is the difference between null and undefined?
1. `null` represents no value, while `undefined` represents an uninitialized variable.
2. Both are the same in JavaScript.
3. `null` is a keyword, and `undefined` is not.
4. `undefined` is an object, and `null` is not.

Answer: 1. `null` represents no value, while `undefined` represents an uninitialized variable.
Explanation: `null` explicitly represents "nothing," while `undefined` is the default value for uninitialized variables.

What will the following code output?
```
let x = 10;
{
  const x = 20;
  console.log(x);
}
console.log(x);
```
1. 10 and 10
2. 20 and 10
3. 20 and 20
4. `Error`

Answer: 2. 20 and 10
Explanation: The `const` x inside the block is block-scoped and does not affect the outer `let` x.

JavaScript Comments and Code Organization

1. Introduction to Comments

Comments in JavaScript are notes that help developers document code, explain logic, and improve code readability. They are ignored by the JavaScript engine and do not affect the program's execution.

Types of Comments

Single-line comments: Start with //.

```
// This is a single-line comment
let x = 10; // Assigning 10 to x
```

Multi-line comments: Enclosed in /* ... */.

```
/*
    This is a multi-line comment.
    It spans multiple lines.
*/
let y = 20;
```

2. Benefits of Using Comments

- Enhance code readability.
- Explain complex logic.
- Provide information about code functionality.
- Act as placeholders for future code.
- Disable code temporarily during debugging.

3. Best Practices for Comments

- Keep comments concise and relevant.
- Use comments to explain "why," not "what."
- Avoid redundant comments.
- Use proper formatting for consistency.

```
// Bad comment: Explains what is obvious
```

```
let total = 10 + 20; // Adds 10 and 20
// Good comment: Explains why the operation
is necessary
let total = 10 + 20; // Calculating the
total score for level completion
```

4. Organizing JavaScript Code

- Write modular code: Break functionality into reusable functions.
- Use meaningful variable and function names.
- Group related code logically.
- Follow consistent indentation and spacing.
- Use comments to structure your code.

```
// Function to calculate the area of a
rectangle
function calculateArea(length, width) {
  return length * width; // Formula for
area
}
// Function to display the area
function displayArea(area) {
  console.log(`The area is ${area}`);
}
// Main program execution
const length = 10; // Rectangle length
const width = 5;    // Rectangle width
const area = calculateArea(length, width);
// Calculate area
displayArea(area); // Display area
```

5. Code Formatting

- Use consistent indentation (2 or 4 spaces).
- Limit line length (e.g., 80–100 characters).
- Use blank lines to separate logical sections.

6. Debugging with Comments

Comments can help debug by temporarily disabling problematic code:

```
// console.log("This line is disabled
temporarily for debugging.");
console.log("Testing other lines of
code.");
```

Multiple-Choice Questions

What symbol is used to start a single-line comment in JavaScript?

1. #
2. //
3. /*
4. --

Answer: 2. //
Explanation: Single-line comments in JavaScript start with //.

Which of the following is the correct syntax for a multi-line comment in JavaScript?

1. <!-- Comment -->
2. /* Comment */
3. // Comment //
4. # Comment #

Answer: 2. `/* Comment */`
Explanation: Multi-line comments in JavaScript are enclosed between `/*` and `*/`.

What is the primary purpose of comments in JavaScript?
1. To make the program run faster.
2. To store data.
3. To explain code to developers.
4. To prevent errors.

Answer: 3. To explain code to developers.
Explanation: Comments are used to document and explain code for better understanding.

Which of the following is NOT a benefit of comments?
1. Explaining complex logic.
2. Enhancing code readability.
3. Slowing down program execution.
4. Providing information about code functionality.

Answer: 3. Slowing down program execution.
Explanation: Comments do not affect program execution since they are ignored by the JavaScript engine.

How can comments be used in debugging?
1. By explaining errors.
2. By disabling specific lines of code.
3. By slowing down the program.
4. By removing all variables.

Answer: 2. By disabling specific lines of code.
Explanation: Comments can be used to temporarily disable problematic lines during debugging.

What will the following code output?

```
// console.log("Hello");
console.log("World");
```

1. `"Hello"`
2. `"World"`
3. `"Hello"` `"World"`
4. No output

Answer: 2. `"World"`
Explanation: The first line is a comment and is ignored; only the second line executes.

Which of the following is considered a best practice for comments?
1. Writing comments for every line of code.
2. Using comments to explain why, not what.
3. Keeping comments as detailed as possible, regardless of relevance.
4. Avoiding comments altogether.

Answer: 2. Using comments to explain why, not what.
Explanation: Comments should focus on explaining the reasoning behind code rather than stating obvious facts.

What will happen if you use // to comment a block of code?
1. It will comment out the entire block.
2. It will comment only the first line.
3. It will throw an error.
4. It will leave the block unchanged.

Answer: 2. It will comment only the first line.
Explanation: The // symbol works for single-line comments only.

What is the correct way to write a multi-line comment?
1.
```
/* This is
a multi-line
comment */
```

2.
```
<!-- This is
a multi-line
comment -->
```
3.
```
# This is
a multi-line
comment #
```
4.
```
// This is
a multi-line
comment //
```
Answer: 1.
```
/* This is
a multi-line
comment */
```
Explanation: Multi-line comments in JavaScript use the `/*` `... */` syntax.

Which of the following is NOT a use of comments?
1. To document code.
2. To add logic to the program.
3. To temporarily disable code.
4. To explain functionality.

Answer: 2. To add logic to the program.
Explanation: Comments are ignored by the JavaScript engine and do not add logic to the program.

What will this code output?
```
/*
console.log("Hello");
*/
```

```
console.log("World");
```
1. "Hello"
2. "World"
3. "Hello" "World"
4. No output

Answer: 2. "World"
Explanation: The multi-line comment disables the first `console.log` statement.

What is the main reason for organizing code into sections using comments?
1. To run the code faster.
2. To make debugging easier.
3. To confuse other developers.
4. To reduce memory usage.

Answer: 2. To make debugging easier.
Explanation: Well-organized code with comments helps developers understand and debug code faster.

Which of these is an example of a redundant comment?
1.
```
let sum = 10 + 20; // Adds 10 and 20
let sum = 10 + 20; // Calculates total score
// This is a placeholder for future logic
let sum = 10 + 20;
/* Complex calculation starts here */
let sum = 10 + 20;
```
Answer: 1.
```
let sum = 10 + 20; // Adds 10 and 20
```
Explanation: This comment repeats what the code already makes obvious.

What happens if you use comments excessively in your code?
1. It improves execution speed.
2. It increases code readability.
3. It makes the code cluttered.
4. It reduces memory usage.

Answer: 3. It makes the code cluttered.
Explanation: Overusing comments can make code harder to read and understand.

Which is NOT a valid use of comments?
1. Documenting functions.
2. Adding error handling logic.
3. Explaining complex algorithms.
4. Disabling specific lines of code.

Answer: 2. Adding error handling logic.
Explanation: Comments are not executable and cannot add logic to the code.

What is a common use of comments when working in teams?
1. To confuse team members.
2. To document the purpose of code for better collaboration.
3. To remove unnecessary code.
4. To add variables for debugging.

Answer: 2. To document the purpose of code for better collaboration.
Explanation: Comments help explain the code's purpose, making it easier for team members to understand and maintain.

Which of the following would be considered well-commented code?

1.
```
let x = 10; // Variable for storing data
```

```
2. let x = 10; // This variable stores
   the user ID for tracking purposes
3. let x = 10; // This is x
4. let x = 10;
```

Answer: 2.

```
let x = 10; // This variable stores the
user ID for tracking purposes
```

Explanation: This comment provides useful context about the variable's purpose without being redundant.

How can you disable a block of code without deleting it?

1. Wrap it in a multi-line comment.
2. Place a # at the beginning of each line.
3. Delete the code and rewrite it later.
4. Place a /* at the start and */ at the end of the block.

Answer: 4. Place a /* at the start and */ at the end of the block.
Explanation: Multi-line comments (/* ... */) can be used to disable a block of code temporarily.

What is the output of this code?

```
// let x = 5;
// let y = 10;
console.log(x + y);
```

1. 15
2. undefined
3. NaN
4. Error

Answer: 4. Error
Explanation: Both variables x and y are commented out, so they are undefined, and the code throws an error.

Which of the following is true about JavaScript comments?

1. They are included in the final output of the code.
2. They can execute code.
3. They are ignored by the JavaScript engine during execution.
4. They can only be single-line.

Answer: 3. They are ignored by the JavaScript engine during execution.
Explanation: Comments are non-executable and are not processed by the JavaScript engine.

Which comment style is best for temporarily disabling one or two lines of code?

1. Multi-line comment (/* ... */)
2. Single-line comment (//)
3. HTML comment (<!-- ... -->)
4. None of the above

Answer: 2. Single-line comment (//)
Explanation: Single-line comments (//) are ideal for temporarily disabling a few lines of code.

Why should comments not describe obvious code?

1. To save memory.
2. To avoid redundancy and maintain focus on meaningful explanations.
3. To confuse other developers.
4. To make the code faster.

Answer: 2. To avoid redundancy and maintain focus on meaningful explanations.
Explanation: Redundant comments add clutter and do not enhance understanding.

What is the best way to comment a placeholder for future code?

1.

```
let placeholder; // Variable to be used in
future development
// TODO: Implement the functionality here
/*
   This section needs more work.
*/
```

4.   All of the above

Answer: 4. All of the above

Explanation: All options provide meaningful placeholders, but using a TODO comment is a standard practice.

What happens if you comment out a return statement in a function?

1. The function stops working.
2. The function always returns undefined.
3. The function executes normally.
4. The function throws an error.

Answer: 2. The function always returns undefined.

Explanation: If a return statement is commented out, the function does not return any value, resulting in undefined.

What will the following code output?

```
let x = 10;
let y = 20;
/* console.log(x); */
console.log(y);
```

1. 10
2. 20
3. 10 20

4. undefined

Answer: 2. 20

Explanation: The first `console.log` is commented out, so only the second statement is executed.

JavaScript Operators

1. Arithmetic Operators

Arithmetic operators are used to perform mathematical calculations in JavaScript.

Operator	Description	Example	Result
+	Addition	5 + 2	7
-	Subtraction	5 - 2	3
*	Multiplication	5 * 2	10
/	Division	10 / 2	5
%	Modulus (remainder)	10 % 3	1
**	Exponentiation (Power)	2 ** 3	8

2. Assignment Operators

Assignment operators assign values to variables.

Operator	Description	Example	Result

=	Assign	x = 5	x is 5
+=	Add and assign	x += 3	x = x + 3
-=	Subtract and assign	x -= 2	x = x - 2
*=	Multiply and assign	x *= 2	x = x * 2
/=	Divide and assign	x /= 2	x = x / 2
%=	Modulus and assign	x %= 2	x = x % 2
**=	Exponentiation and assign	x **= 2	x = x ** 2

3. Comparison Operators

Comparison operators are used to compare two values and return a Boolean (true or false).

Operator	Description	Example	Result
==	Equal to (value)	5 == '5'	true
===	Strict equal to (value and type)	5 === '5'	false

!=	Not equal to (value)	5 != '5'	false
!==	Strict not equal to (value and type)	5 !== '5'	true
>	Greater than	10 > 5	true
<	Less than	10 < 5	false
>=	Greater than or equal to	10 >= 10	true
<=	Less than or equal to	10 <= 5	false

4. Operator Precedence

Operator precedence determines the order in which operations are performed.

Precedence Level	Operators
Highest	( ) (Parentheses)
2nd Highest	** (Exponentiation)
3rd Highest	*, /, %
4th Highest	+, -
Lowest	Assignment (=)

Example:

```
let result = 5 + 2 * 3; // 11
(Multiplication is performed first)
result = (5 + 2) * 3;    // 21 (Parentheses
are evaluated first)
```

Multiple-Choice Questions

What will the following code output?
```
console.log(5 + 3 * 2);
```
    1. 16
    2. 11
    3. 13
    4. 10

Answer: 2. 11
Explanation: Multiplication has higher precedence than addition, so 3 * 2 is evaluated first, followed by 5 + 6.

Which operator is used to find the remainder of a division?
    1. /
    2. %
    3. **
    4. //

Answer: 2. %
Explanation: The modulus operator % returns the remainder of a division.

What is the result of 5 ** 2?
    1. 25
    2. 10
    3. 7
    4. 32

Answer: 1. 25
Explanation: The ** operator raises the first number to the power of the second ($5^2 = 25$).

What will this code output?
```
let x = 10;
x += 5;
console.log(x);
```
   1. 10
   2. 15
   3. 5
   4. undefined

Answer: 2. 15
Explanation: The += operator adds 5 to the current value of x.

What is the result of the following comparison?
```
console.log(5 == "5");
```
   1. true
   2. false
   3. undefined
   4. Error

Answer: 1. true
Explanation: The == operator compares values only, not types, so the result is true.

What will the following code output?
```
console.log(5 === "5");
```
   1. true
   2. false
   3. undefined
   4. Error

Answer: 2. `false`
Explanation: The `===` operator compares both value and type, so 5 (number) is not equal to "5" (string).

Which operator increases a value by 1?

1. +
2. +=
3. ++
4. =

Answer: 3. ++
Explanation: The increment operator (++) increases a variable's value by 1.

What is the result of 10 % 3?

1. 1
2. 2
3. 3
4. 10

Answer: 1. 1
Explanation: The modulus operator (%) returns the remainder of 10 / 3, which is 1.

What will the following code output?
```
let x = 5;
let y = 10;
console.log(x > y);
```
1. `true`
2. `false`
3. `undefined`
4. `Error`

Answer: 2. `false`
Explanation: The > operator checks if x is greater than y. Since 5 is not greater than 10, the result is `false`.

Which of these is a comparison operator?
1. `*`
2. `+=`
3. `===`
4. `**`

Answer: 3. `===`
Explanation: The === operator checks for strict equality (both value and type).

What will the following code output?
```
let x = 10;
console.log(x <= 10);
```
1. `true`
2. `false`
3. `undefined`
4. `Error`

Answer: 1. `true`
Explanation: The <= operator checks if x is less than or equal to 10, which is `true`.

What will this code output?
```
let x = 5;
x *= 2;
console.log(x);
```
1. 5
2. 10
3. 25
4. 2

Answer: 2. 10
Explanation: The *= operator multiplies x by 2, resulting in 10.

Which operator is used for exponentiation?
1. **
2. ^
3. //
4. *

Answer: 1. **
Explanation: The ** operator is used for exponentiation in JavaScript.

What is the result of 10 != "10"?
1. true
2. false
3. undefined
4. Error

Answer: 2. false
Explanation: The ! = operator checks for inequality of value. Since the values are the same, the result is false.

What will the following code output?
```
console.log(7 > 5 && 5 > 10);
```
1. true
2. false
3. undefined
4. Error

Answer: 2. false
Explanation: The logical AND (&&) operator returns false if any condition is false.

What will the following code output?

```
let a = 3;
let b = 2;
console.log(a > b || b > 5);
```

    1. true

    2. false

    3. undefined

    4. Error

Answer: 1. true

Explanation: The logical OR (||) operator returns true if at least one condition is true. Here, a > b is true, so the result is true.

What is the result of the following code?

```
let x = 8;
x %= 3;
console.log(x);
```

    1. 2

    2. 3

    3. 8

    4. 5

Answer: 1. 2

Explanation: The modulus assignment operator (%=) calculates the remainder of x / 3. The result is 2.

Which operator compares both value and type?

    1. ==

    2. ===

    3. =

    4. !=

Answer: 2. ===

Explanation: The strict equality operator (===) compares both value and type.

What will the following code output?

```
console.log(5 !== "5");
```

   1. true
   2. false
   3. undefined
   4. Error

Answer: 1. true

Explanation: The strict inequality operator (!==) checks if value or type are not equal. Since the types differ, the result is true.

What does this code output?

```
let x = 5 + 10 * 2;
console.log(x);
```

   1. 30
   2. 25
   3. 20
   4. 15

Answer: 2. 25

Explanation: Multiplication has higher precedence than addition, so 10 * 2 is calculated first, resulting in 5 + 20.

What will the following code output?

```
let a = 10;
let b = 5;
console.log(a < b && b > 0);
```

   1. true
   2. false

3. undefined

4. Error

Answer: 2. false
Explanation: The logical AND (&&) operator returns false
if any condition is false. Since a < b is false, the result
is false.

What will the following code output?

```
let result = 10 / 2 + 3 * 2;
console.log(result);
```

1. 11

2. 13

3. 14

4. 15

Answer: 1. 11
Explanation: Operator precedence applies: 3 * 2 is 6,
then 10 / 2 is 5, and finally 5 + 6 is 11.

What is the result of this code?

```
let a = 4;
let b = 4;
console.log(a <= b);
```

1. true

2. false

3. undefined

4. Error

Answer: 1. true
Explanation: The less than or equal to operator (<=)
checks if a is less than or equal to b. Since both are equal,
the result is true.

What does this code output?

```
let x = 5;
x -= 2;
console.log(x);
```

    1. 3

    2. 5

    3. 7

    4. 2

Answer: 1. 3

Explanation: The -= operator subtracts 2 from x, so x becomes 3.

What is the result of the following code?

```
let x = (5 + 3) * 2;
console.log(x);
```

    1. 10

    2. 16

    3. 20

    4. 15

Answer: 2. 16

Explanation: Parentheses have the highest precedence, so 5 + 3 is calculated first (8), followed by multiplication with 2.

Logical Operators in JavaScript

Logical operators in JavaScript are used to combine or invert Boolean values. They are commonly used in conditions and expressions to determine the logic of a program.

1. The AND Operator (&&)

The AND operator returns `true` only if **both** operands are `true`. If either operand is `false`, the result is `false`.

Operand 1	Operand 2	Result
true	true	true
true	false	false
false	true	false
false	false	false

Example:

```
let age = 25;
let hasLicense = true;
if (age >= 18 && hasLicense) {
   console.log("You can drive!"); // Both
conditions are true
} else {
   console.log("You cannot drive.");
}
```

2. The OR Operator (||)

The OR operator returns `true` if **either** operand is `true`. It returns `false` only if **both** operands are `false`.

Operand 1	Operand 2	Result
true	true	true

true	false	true
false	true	true
false	false	false

Example:

```
let hasCash = false;
let hasCreditCard = true;
if (hasCash || hasCreditCard) {
  console.log("You can make a purchase!");
// At least one condition is true
} else {
  console.log("You cannot make a
purchase.");
}
```

3. The NOT Operator (!)

The NOT operator inverts a Boolean value. If the value is true, it returns false, and vice versa.

Operand	Result
true	false
false	true

Example:

```
let isRaining = false;
if (!isRaining) {
  console.log("You don't need an
umbrella!"); // Inverts false to true
```

```
} else {
  console.log("Take an umbrella.");
}
```

4. Logical Operators with Non-Boolean Values

Logical operators can also work with non-Boolean values. JavaScript evaluates them based on their **truthy** or **falsy** nature:

- **Falsy values**: `false`, `0`, `" "` (empty string), `null`, `undefined`, NaN
- **Truthy values**: All other values (e.g., non-zero numbers, non-empty strings, objects)

Example with &&:

```
console.log(0 && "Hello"); // Outputs: 0
(short-circuits at the first falsy value)
console.log(1 && "Hello"); // Outputs:
"Hello" (both values are truthy)
```

Example with | |:

```
console.log(null || "Hello"); // Outputs:
"Hello" (returns the first truthy value)
console.log("Hi" || "Hello"); // Outputs:
"Hi" (first value is truthy)
```

5. Operator Precedence

Logical operators have precedence:

1. **NOT (!)**: Highest
2. **AND (&&)**
3. **OR (| |)**: Lowest

Example:

```
let result = true || false && false;
console.log(result); // Outputs: true (AND
is evaluated first, then OR)
```

To control the evaluation, use parentheses:

```
let result = (true || false) && false;
console.log(result); // Outputs: false
```

Multiple-Choice Questions

What is the result of this code?
```
console.log(true && false);
```
1. true
2. false
3. undefined
4. Error

Answer: 2. false
Explanation: The AND operator (&&) requires both operands to be true. Since one is false, the result is false.

What does the following code output?
```
console.log(false || true);
```
1. true
2. false
3. undefined
4. Error

Answer: 1. true
Explanation: The OR operator (||) returns true if at least one operand is true.

What will this code output?
```
console.log(!true);
```
1. true
2. false
3. undefined
4. Error

Answer: 2. `false`
Explanation: The NOT operator (`!`) inverts the value of `true` to `false`.

What does the following code output?
```
let a = 5 > 3 && 10 > 7;
console.log(a);
```
1. `true`
2. `false`
3. `undefined`
4. `Error`

Answer: 1. `true`
Explanation: Both conditions are `true`, so the AND operator returns `true`.

Which of the following expressions evaluates to true?
1. `false && true`
2. `true || false`
3. `!false && false`
4. `false || false`

Answer: 2. `true || false`
Explanation: The OR operator (`||`) returns `true` if at least one operand is `true`.

What is the result of this code?
```
console.log(0 || "Hello");
```
1. `0`
2. `"Hello"`
3. `undefined`
4. `Error`

Answer: 2. `"Hello"`
Explanation: The OR operator returns the first truthy value. Since 0 is falsy, it returns `"Hello"`.

What will this code output?
```
console.log(!0);
```
1. `true`
2. `false`
3. `undefined`
4. `Error`

Answer: 1. `true`
Explanation: The NOT operator inverts the falsy value 0 to `true`.

What is the result of this expression?
```
console.log(false || 0);
```
1. `false`
2. `0`
3. `undefined`
4. `Error`

Answer: 2. `0`
Explanation: The OR operator returns the first truthy value. Since both operands are falsy, it returns 0.

What is the output of this code?
```
console.log(5 && 0 && "Hello");
```
1. `5`
2. `0`
3. `"Hello"`
4. `undefined`

Answer: 2. 0
Explanation: The AND operator short-circuits and returns the first falsy value, which is 0.

What does this code output?

```
console.log(10 > 5 || 5 > 10 && 5 === 5);
```

1. true
2. false
3. undefined
4. Error

Answer: 1. true
Explanation: AND has higher precedence than OR. The expression evaluates as (10 > 5) || (false && true), which simplifies to true.

Question 11
What does this code output?

```
console.log(!(10 > 5));
```

1. true
2. false
3. undefined
4. Error

Answer: 2. false
Explanation: The expression 10 > 5 evaluates to true. The NOT operator (!) inverts true to false.

What is the result of this expression?

```
console.log(true && false || true);
```

1. true
2. false
3. undefined
4. Error

Answer: 1. `true`
Explanation: The AND operator (&&) has higher precedence than OR (||). The expression evaluates as (`true && false`) `|| true`, which simplifies to `false || true` and results in `true`.

What will this code output?
```
let a = true;
let b = false;
console.log(a || b && !a);
```
1. `true`
2. `false`
3. `undefined`
4. `Error`

Answer: 1. `true`
Explanation: The AND (&&) operator has higher precedence than OR (||). The expression evaluates as `a || (b && !a)`, which simplifies to `true || (false && false)`, resulting in `true`.

What does this code output?
```
console.log(0 && "Hello" || "World");
```
1. `0`
2. `"Hello"`
3. `"World"`
4. `undefined`

Answer: 3. `"World"`
Explanation: The AND operator (&&) short-circuits at `0` (falsy), so the OR operator (||) evaluates the next operand, which is `"World"`.

What is the output of the following code?
```
console.log(!false || false);
```

1. true
2. false
3. undefined
4. Error

Answer: 1. `true`
Explanation: The NOT operator (`!`) inverts `false` to `true`. The OR operator (`||`) then evaluates as `true || false`, which is `true`.

What does this code output?
```
console.log(5 && 10 || 0);
```
1. 5
2. 10
3. 0
4. undefined

Answer: 2. `10`
Explanation: The AND operator (`&&`) evaluates to `10` (the second truthy value), and the OR operator (`||`) short-circuits at the first truthy value, which is `10`.

What is the result of this expression?
```
console.log(!null && "Yes");
```
1. true
2. "Yes"
3. null
4. undefined

Answer: 2. `"Yes"`
Explanation: The NOT operator (`!`) converts `null` (falsy) to `true`. The AND operator (`&&`) then evaluates the second operand, `"Yes"`.

What does this code output?

```
console.log(false || !0);
```

1. true
2. false
3. undefined
4. Error

Answer: 1. true

Explanation: The NOT operator (!) converts 0 (falsy) to true. The OR operator (||) evaluates as false || true, resulting in true.

What will this code output?

```
console.log("Hello" && 0 && "World");
```

1. "Hello"
2. 0
3. "World"
4. undefined

Answer: 2. 0

Explanation: The AND operator (&&) short-circuits at the first falsy value, which is 0.

What does this code output?

```
console.log(1 || 2 && 3);
```

1. 1
2. 3
3. 2
4. undefined

Answer: 1. 1

Explanation: The AND operator (&&) has higher precedence than OR (||). The expression evaluates as 1 || (2 && 3). Since 1 is truthy, the OR operator short-circuits and returns 1.

What is the result of this expression?

```
console.log(10 > 5 && 5 > 10 || 5 === 5);
```

1. `true`
2. `false`
3. `undefined`
4. `Error`

Answer: 1. `true`
Explanation: The AND operator evaluates as `10 > 5 &&`
`false`, which is `false`. The OR operator then evaluates
`false || true`, resulting in `true`.

What does this code output?

```
let x = null || undefined || "Default";
console.log(x);
```

1. `null`
2. `undefined`
3. `"Default"`
4. `Error`

Answer: 3. `"Default"`
Explanation: The OR operator returns the first truthy
value. Both `null` and `undefined` are falsy, so it returns
`"Default"`.

What will this code output?

```
console.log(!undefined && "Yes");
```

1. `true`
2. `"Yes"`
3. `undefined`
4. `Error`

Answer: 2. `"Yes"`
Explanation: The NOT operator converts `undefined`

(falsy) to `true`. The AND operator then evaluates as `true && "Yes"`, resulting in `"Yes"`.

What is the result of this code?

```
console.log(!(5 > 10 || 10 > 5));
```

1. `true`
2. `false`
3. `undefined`
4. `Error`

Answer: 2. `false`
Explanation: The OR operator evaluates as `false || true`, which is `true`. The NOT operator inverts this to `false`.

What does this code output?

```
console.log(false && true || true && false);
```

1. `true`
2. `false`
3. `undefined`
4. `Error`

Answer: 2. `false`
Explanation: The AND operators evaluate first. The expression becomes `false || false`, resulting in `false`.

JavaScript if/else Statements

1. What are if/else Statements?

`if/else` statements in JavaScript are used to perform conditional execution of code. They allow developers to execute different blocks of code based on whether a specified condition evaluates to `true` or `false`.

2. Syntax of if/else Statements

Basic `if` Statement:
```
if (condition) {
    // Code to execute if condition is true
}
```

`if/else` Statement:
```
if (condition) {
    // Code to execute if condition is true
} else {
    // Code to execute if condition is false
}
```

`if/else if/else` Statement:
```
if (condition1) {
    // Code to execute if condition1 is true
} else if (condition2) {
    // Code to execute if condition2 is true
} else {
    // Code to execute if neither condition1
nor condition2 is true
}
```

3. Conditional Expressions

The condition inside an `if` statement must evaluate to a Boolean value (`true` or `false`). Commonly used expressions include:

Comparison Operators: <, <=, >, >=, ==, !=, ===, !==
```
if (age >= 18) {
    console.log("You are an adult.");
}
```
Logical Operators: &&, ||, !
```
if (age >= 18 && hasID) {
```

```
  console.log("You can enter.");
}
```

4. Nested if/else Statements

You can nest `if` statements inside each other for more complex logic:

```
if (age >= 18) {
  if (hasLicense) {
    console.log("You can drive.");
  } else {
    console.log("You need a license to
drive.");
  }
} else {
  console.log("You are too young to
drive.");
}
```

5. Ternary Operator

The ternary operator is a shorthand for `if/else` statements:

```
let result = condition ? valueIfTrue :
valueIfFalse;
```

Example:

```
let message = age >= 18 ? "Adult" :
"Minor";
console.log(message);
```

6. Truthy and Falsy Values

JavaScript evaluates certain values as truthy or falsy:

- **Falsy values**: `false`, `0`, `" "` (empty string), `null`, `undefined`, NaN

- **Truthy values**: All other values (e.g., non-zero numbers, non-empty strings)

Example:

```
if (0) {
  console.log("This won't run because 0 is falsy.");
} else {
  console.log("This will run.");
}
```

Multiple-Choice Questions

What is the output of this code?

```
let age = 20;
if (age >= 18) {
  console.log("Adult");
} else {
  console.log("Minor");
}
```

1. Adult
2. Minor
3. undefined
4. Error

Answer: 1. Adult

Explanation: The condition age >= 18 evaluates to true, so the if block is executed.

Which of the following is a valid if statement?

1. if x > 5 { console.log("Yes"); }
2. if (x > 5) console.log("Yes");
3. if (x > 5) { console.log("Yes"); }
4. Both 2 and 3

Answer: 4. Both 2 and 3
Explanation: Parentheses are required for the condition. Curly braces are optional if the `if` block has only one statement.

What does this code output?

```
let x = 5;
if (x > 10) {
  console.log("Greater");
} else {
  console.log("Smaller");
}
```

1. Greater
2. Smaller
3. undefined
4. Error

Answer: 2. Smaller
Explanation: The condition `x > 10` evaluates to `false`, so the `else` block is executed.

Which operator is used to check for equality of value and type?

1. `=`
2. `==`
3. `===`
4. `!=`

Answer: 3. `===`
Explanation: The `===` operator checks for both value and type equality.

What does this code output?

```
let x = 10;
if (x > 5 && x < 15) {
```

```
    console.log("Within range");
} else {
    console.log("Out of range");
}
```

1. Within range
2. Out of range
3. undefined
4. Error

Answer: 1. Within range
Explanation: Both conditions x > 5 and x < 15 are true, so the if block is executed.

What is the output of this code?
```
let name = "";
if (name) {
    console.log("Valid name");
} else {
    console.log("Invalid name");
}
```

1. Valid name
2. Invalid name
3. undefined
4. Error

Answer: 2. Invalid name
Explanation: An empty string is falsy, so the else block is executed.

What is the purpose of an else if statement?

1. To check additional conditions if the if condition is false.
2. To execute code if the if condition is true.
3. To stop code execution.

4. To debug code.

Answer: 1. To check additional conditions if the `if` condition is false.

Explanation: `else if` is used to provide additional conditions when the previous `if` condition fails.

What is the output of this code?

```
let x = 7;
if (x > 10) {
  console.log("A");
} else if (x > 5) {
  console.log("B");
} else {
  console.log("C");
}
```

1. A
2. B
3. C
4. Error

Answer: 2. B

Explanation: The condition x > 10 is false, but x > 5 is true, so the `else if` block executes.

What is the output of this code?

```
let num = 0;
if (!num) {
  console.log("Falsy value");
} else {
  console.log("Truthy value");
}
```

1. Falsy value

2. Truthy value
3. undefined
4. Error

Answer: 1. Falsy value
Explanation: The NOT operator (!) inverts 0 (falsy) to true, so the if block executes.

What will this code output?

```
let age = 18;
let message = age >= 18 ? "Adult" :
"Minor";
console.log(message);
```

1. Adult
2. Minor
3. undefined
4. Error

Answer: 1. Adult
Explanation: The ternary operator checks if age >= 18 is true, and assigns "Adult" to message.

What is the result of this code?

```
let x = 10;
if (x % 2 === 0) {
  console.log("Even");
} else {
  console.log("Odd");
}
```

1. Even
2. Odd
3. undefined
4. Error

Answer: 1. Even
Explanation: The condition x % 2 === 0 checks if the number is divisible by 2. Since 10 is even, the if block executes.

What does this code output?

```
let num = 15;
if (num > 10) {
  if (num < 20) {
    console.log("Between 10 and 20");
  }
}
```

    1. Between 10 and 20
    2. undefined
    3. Error
    4. No output

Answer: 1. Between 10 and 20
Explanation: Both conditions num > 10 and num < 20 are true, so the nested if block executes.

What is the output of this code?

```
let x = "5";
if (x == 5) {
  console.log("Equal value");
} else {
  console.log("Not equal");
}
```

    1. Equal value
    2. Not equal
    3. undefined
    4. Error

Answer: 1. `Equal value`
Explanation: The `==` operator compares values without checking types. Since `"5"` and 5 have equal values, the `if` block executes.

Which statement is true about else blocks?
1. They must always follow an `if` block.
2. They can execute only if the `if` condition is true.
3. They execute when the `if` condition is false.
4. They are mandatory in an `if`/`else` statement.

Answer: 3. They execute when the `if` condition is false.
Explanation: The `else` block executes when the `if` condition is false.

What does this code output?
```
let x = 5;
if (x > 5) {
   console.log("Greater");
} else if (x === 5) {
   console.log("Equal");
} else {
   console.log("Smaller");
}
```
1. `Greater`
2. `Equal`
3. `Smaller`
4. `Error`

Answer: 2. `Equal`
Explanation: The `if` condition is false, but the `else if` condition x `===` 5 is true, so the `else if` block executes.

What will this code output?

```javascript
let isLoggedIn = false;
if (!isLoggedIn) {
  console.log("Please log in.");
} else {
  console.log("Welcome!");
}
```

    1. Please log in.

    2. Welcome!

    3. undefined

    4. Error

Answer: 1. Please log in.

Explanation: The NOT operator (!) inverts false to true, so the if block executes.

What is the output of this code?

```javascript
let num = 0;
if (num) {
  console.log("Truthy");
} else {
  console.log("Falsy");
}
```

    1. Truthy

    2. Falsy

    3. undefined

    4. Error

Answer: 2. Falsy

Explanation: 0 is a falsy value in JavaScript, so the else block executes.

What does this code output?

```
let age = 25;
if (age > 18) {
  console.log("Adult");
} else if (age > 12) {
  console.log("Teenager");
} else {
  console.log("Child");
}
```

    1. Adult
    2. Teenager
    3. Child
    4. undefined

Answer: 1. Adult
Explanation: The first condition age > 18 is true, so the if block executes, and no further conditions are checked.

Which of the following is a valid if statement?
    1. if (x > 5) {}
    2. if x > 5 {}
    3. if (x > 5)
    4. Both 1 and 3

Answer: 1. if (x > 5) {}
Explanation: The condition in an if statement must be enclosed in parentheses, and curly braces are required for multiple statements.

What is the result of this code?

```
let x = 10;
if (x < 10) {
  console.log("Less");
} else {
```

```
    console.log("Greater or Equal");
}
```
    1. Less
    2. Greater or Equal
    3. undefined
    4. Error

Answer: 2. `Greater or Equal`
Explanation: The condition `x < 10` is false, so the `else` block executes.

What does this code output?
```
let isMember = true;
let discount = isMember ? "10%" : "0%";
console.log(discount);
```
    1. 10%
    2. 0%
    3. undefined
    4. Error

Answer: 1. 10%
Explanation: The ternary operator evaluates `isMember` as `true`, so `"10%"` is assigned to `discount`.

What does this code output?
```
let x = 8;
if (x % 2 === 0) {
  console.log("Even");
} else {
  console.log("Odd");
}
```
    1. Even
    2. Odd

3. undefined

4. Error

Answer: 1. Even

Explanation: The condition x % 2 === 0 checks if x is divisible by 2. Since 8 is even, the if block executes.

What does this code output?

```
if ("Hello") {
  console.log("Truthy");
} else {
  console.log("Falsy");
}
```

1. Truthy

2. Falsy

3. undefined

4. Error

Answer: 1. Truthy

Explanation: Non-empty strings are truthy in JavaScript, so the if block executes.

What does this code output?

```
let x = null;
if (x) {
  console.log("Truthy");
} else {
  console.log("Falsy");
}
```

1. Truthy

2. Falsy

3. undefined

4. Error

Answer: 2. `Falsy`
Explanation: `null` is a falsy value, so the `else` block executes.

What does this code output?
```
let x = 3;
if (x > 2) {
  if (x < 5) {
    console.log("Between 2 and 5");
  }
}
```
1. `Between 2 and 5`
2. `undefined`
3. `Error`
4. No output

Answer: 1. `Between 2 and 5`
Explanation: Both conditions `x > 2` and `x < 5` are true, so the nested `if` block executes.

JavaScript switch Statements

1. What is a switch Statement?

The `switch` statement is used to execute one block of code out of many based on a matching case. It provides an alternative to multiple `if/else if` statements, making the code easier to read and maintain.

2. Syntax of switch
```
switch (expression) {
  case value1:
    // Code to execute if expression ===
value1
```

```
    break;
  case value2:
    // Code to execute if expression ===
value2
    break;
  default:
    // Code to execute if no case matches
}
```

- **expression**: The value to be compared against each case.
- **case value1**: A possible match for the expression.
- **break**: Prevents execution from continuing into the next case.
- **default**: Executes if no case matches (optional).

3. Key Points about switch Statements

- **Strict Comparison (===)**: switch uses strict comparison, so 5 (number) is not equal to "5" (string).
- **break Statement**: Without break, the execution "falls through" to the next case.
- **default Case**: Acts as a catch-all for unmatched cases and is optional.

4. Example of a switch Statement

```
let day = 3;
switch (day) {
  case 1:
    console.log("Monday");
    break;
  case 2:
```

```
    console.log("Tuesday");
    break;
  case 3:
    console.log("Wednesday");
    break;
  default:
    console.log("Invalid day");
}
```
Output: Wednesday

5. Example Without break

```
let color = "red";
switch (color) {
  case "red":
    console.log("Stop");
  case "yellow":
    console.log("Slow down");
  case "green":
    console.log("Go");
}
```
Output:
```
Stop
Slow down
Go
```
Explanation: Without break, execution continues to the next cases.

6. Grouping Cases

You can group cases to execute the same block of code:

```
let grade = "B";
switch (grade) {
```

```
  case "A":
  case "B":
    console.log("Good job!");
    break;
  case "C":
    console.log("Average");
    break;
  default:
    console.log("Invalid grade");
}
```
Output: Good job!

Multiple-Choice Questions

What does the following code output?
```
let fruit = "apple";
switch (fruit) {
  case "apple":
    console.log("Apples are red or
green.");
    break;
  case "banana":
    console.log("Bananas are yellow.");
    break;
  default:
    console.log("Unknown fruit.");
}
```
  1. Apples are red or green.
  2. Bananas are yellow.
  3. Unknown fruit.

4. No output

Answer: 1. `Apples are red or green.`
Explanation: The `fruit` value matches the `case` `"apple"`, so its block is executed.

What happens if there is no break in a switch case?
1. It throws an error.
2. Execution stops immediately.
3. Execution continues to the next case.
4. The `default` case is executed.

Answer: 3. Execution continues to the next case.
Explanation: Without `break`, the execution "falls through" to the next case.

What is the purpose of the default case in a switch statement?
1. To exit the `switch`.
2. To handle unmatched cases.
3. To handle errors.
4. To replace the `break` statement.

Answer: 2. To handle unmatched cases.
Explanation: The `default` case executes if no other case matches the `expression`.

What is the output of this code?
```
let day = 6;
switch (day) {
  case 6:
  case 7:
    console.log("Weekend");
    break;
  default:
    console.log("Weekday");
```

```
}
```
   1. Weekend
   2. Weekday
   3. No output
   4. Error

Answer: 1. Weekend
Explanation: The value day = 6 matches the grouped case 6 and case 7.

What will this code output?
```
let value = "5";
switch (value) {
  case 5:
    console.log("Number 5");
    break;
  case "5":
    console.log("String 5");
    break;
  default:
    console.log("Not 5");
}
```
   1. Number 5
   2. String 5
   3. Not 5
   4. Error

Answer: 2. String 5
Explanation: switch uses strict comparison (===), so "5" matches case "5".

What is the output of this code?
```
let x = 10;
```

```
switch (x) {
  case 5:
    console.log("Five");
  case 10:
    console.log("Ten");
  default:
    console.log("Default");
}
```
    1. Ten
    2. Ten Default
    3. Default
    4. No output

Answer: 2. Ten Default

Explanation: Without `break`, execution falls through to the `default` case after `case 10`.

Can the default case appear before all other cases in a switch statement?
    1. Yes
    2. No

Answer: 1. Yes

Explanation: The `default` case can appear anywhere in a `switch` statement but typically appears at the end for readability.

What does this code output?
```
let season = "summer";
switch (season) {
  case "winter":
    console.log("Cold");
    break;
  case "summer":
```

```
      console.log("Hot");
   case "spring":
      console.log("Mild");
      break;
   default:
      console.log("Unknown");
}
```

1. Hot
2. Hot Mild
3. Mild
4. Unknown

Answer: 2. Hot Mild
Explanation: The break is missing after case "summer", so execution falls through to case "spring".

What happens if no case matches and there is no default case?

1. It throws an error.
2. Nothing happens.
3. The last case is executed.
4. The first case is executed.

Answer: 2. Nothing happens.
Explanation: If no case matches and there is no default, the switch statement does nothing.

Which statement is true about switch?

1. It uses loose comparison (==).
2. It uses strict comparison (===).
3. It does not compare values.
4. It only works with numbers.

Answer: 2. It uses strict comparison (===).
Explanation: `switch` uses strict comparison, so both value and type must match.

What will this code output?

```
let grade = "B";
switch (grade) {
  case "A":
    console.log("Excellent");
    break;
  case "B":
  case "C":
    console.log("Good");
    break;
  default:
    console.log("Needs Improvement");
}
```

1. `Excellent`
2. `Good`
3. `Needs Improvement`
4. No output

Answer: 2. Good
Explanation: The value `grade = "B"` matches `case "B"`, and the block executes because it is grouped with `case "C"`.

What happens if a switch statement has no matching cases and no default?

1. It throws an error.
2. It executes all cases.
3. It does nothing.
4. It returns `undefined`.

Answer: 3. It does nothing.
Explanation: If no case matches and there is no `default`, the `switch` statement exits without executing any code.

What is the result of this code?
```
let x = 5;
switch (true) {
  case x < 5:
    console.log("Less than 5");
    break;
  case x === 5:
    console.log("Equal to 5");
    break;
  case x > 5:
    console.log("Greater than 5");
    break;
}
```
1. Less than 5
2. Equal to 5
3. Greater than 5
4. Error

Answer: 2. Equal to 5
Explanation: The `switch` statement uses `true` as the `expression`. The second case matches because `x === 5` evaluates to `true`.

What is the output of this code?
```
let value = "banana";
switch (value) {
  case "apple":
    console.log("Apple");
```

```
case "banana":
  console.log("Banana");
  break;
default:
  console.log("Unknown");
}
```

1. Apple
2. Banana
3. Apple Banana
4. Unknown

Answer: 2. Banana

Explanation: The `value` matches case `"banana"`. Since there is no `break` after case `"apple"`, execution continues to case `"banana"`.

Which of the following statements about switch is true?

1. It can only work with numbers.
2. It uses loose comparison.
3. It can group cases to share the same block.
4. It always requires a `default` case.

Answer: 3. It can group cases to share the same block.
Explanation: Multiple cases can share the same block by grouping them together without a `break` between them.

What does this code output?

```
let num = 3;
switch (num) {
  case 1:
  case 2:
    console.log("Low");
    break;
```

```
case 3:
case 4:
  console.log("Medium");
  break;
default:
  console.log("High");
}
```
1. Low
2. Medium
3. High
4. No output

Answer: 2. Medium
Explanation: The value num = 3 matches case 3, which shares the same block with case 4.

What will this code output?
```
let fruit = "orange";
switch (fruit) {
  case "apple":
    console.log("Apple");
    break;
  case "banana":
    console.log("Banana");
    break;
  default:
    console.log("Unknown fruit");
}
```
1. Apple
2. Banana
3. Unknown fruit
4. No output

Answer: 3. Unknown fruit
Explanation: Since fruit = "orange" does not match any case, the default block executes.

What is the output of this code?
```
let color = "blue";
switch (color) {
  case "red":
    console.log("Red");
  case "blue":
    console.log("Blue");
  default:
    console.log("Unknown color");
}
```
    1. Blue
    2. Blue Unknown color
    3. Unknown color
    4. No output

Answer: 2. Blue Unknown color
Explanation: The break is missing, so execution falls through from case "blue" to the default block.

Can a switch statement evaluate complex conditions like x > 5?
    1. Yes
    2. No

Answer: 1. Yes
Explanation: By using true as the expression in the switch statement, you can evaluate complex conditions in each case.

What happens if multiple cases in a switch match?
    1. The first matching case executes.

2. The last matching case executes.
3. All matching cases execute.
4. It throws an error.

Answer: 1. The first matching case executes.
Explanation: The `switch` statement stops searching for matches after the first matching case.

What does this code output?

```
let day = "Monday";
switch (day) {
  case "Monday":
    console.log("Start of the week");
  case "Friday":
    console.log("End of the workweek");
  default:
    console.log("Another day");
}
```

1. Start of the week
2. Start of the week End of the workweek Another day
3. Another day
4. No output

Answer: 2. Start of the week End of the workweek Another day
Explanation: Without break, execution continues through all cases after a match.

What does this code output?

```
let x = 1;
switch (x) {
  case 0:
    console.log("Zero");
```

```
    break;
  default:
    console.log("Default");
  case 1:
    console.log("One");
    break;
}
```

1. Default One
2. One Default
3. Default
4. One

Answer: 1. Default One
Explanation: Without a break in the default case, execution continues to case 1.

Which is true about using expressions in case values?
1. They must be constants.
2. They can include variables or functions.
3. They cannot be used.
4. They are mandatory.

Answer: 1. They must be constants.
Explanation: case values must be constants, as they are evaluated at compile time.

What does this code output?
```
let weather = "rain";
switch (weather) {
  case "sunny":
    console.log("Wear sunglasses");
    break;
  case "rain":
    console.log("Take an umbrella");
```

```
  default:
    console.log("Check the forecast");
}
```

1. Take an umbrella
2. Take an umbrella Check the forecast
3. Check the forecast
4. No output

Answer: 2. Take an umbrella Check the forecast
Explanation: Without a break after case "rain",
execution falls through to the default case.

What does this code output?

```
let score = 85;
switch (true) {
  case score >= 90:
    console.log("A");
    break;
  case score >= 80:
    console.log("B");
    break;
  case score >= 70:
    console.log("C");
    break;
  default:
    console.log("F");
}
```

1. A
2. B
3. C
4. F

Answer: 2. B

Explanation: The `switch` uses `true` as the expression. The condition `score >= 80` evaluates to `true`, so `case score >= 80` executes.

JavaScript Loops

In JavaScript, loops are used to repeatedly execute a block of code as long as a specified condition evaluates to `true`. There are three primary types of loops: `for`, `while`, and `do...while`.

1. The for Loop

The `for` loop is used when the number of iterations is known beforehand.

Syntax:
```
for (initialization; condition;
increment/decrement) {
   // Code to execute
}
```

Example:
```
for (let i = 1; i <= 5; i++) {
   console.log(i); // Outputs 1, 2, 3, 4, 5
}
```

Key Points:
- **Initialization**: Runs once before the loop starts (e.g., `let i = 0`).
- **Condition**: Checked before each iteration. If `false`, the loop stops.
- **Increment/Decrement**: Updates the loop variable after each iteration.

2. The while Loop

The while loop is used when the number of iterations is not known and depends on a condition.

Syntax:

```
while (condition) {
    // Code to execute
}
```

Example:

```
let i = 1;
while (i <= 5) {
    console.log(i); // Outputs 1, 2, 3, 4, 5
    i++;
}
```

Key Points:

- The loop executes **only if the condition is true** at the beginning of each iteration.
- If the condition is false initially, the loop does not execute.

3. The do...while Loop

The do...while loop is used when the code block must execute at least once, regardless of the condition.

Syntax:

```
do {
    // Code to execute
} while (condition);
```

Example:

```
let i = 1;
do {
    console.log(i); // Outputs 1, 2, 3, 4, 5
    i++;
} while (i <= 5);
```

Key Points:
- Executes the code block **once before checking the condition**.
- Useful when you need the loop to run at least once.

4. Breaking and Continuing in Loops

break: Exits the loop immediately.

```
for (let i = 1; i <= 5; i++) {
  if (i === 3) break; // Stops the loop
when i equals 3
  console.log(i); // Outputs 1, 2
}
```

continue: Skips the current iteration and proceeds to the next one.

```
for (let i = 1; i <= 5; i++) {
  if (i === 3) continue; // Skips the
iteration when i equals 3
  console.log(i); // Outputs 1, 2, 4, 5
}
```

5. Infinite Loops

A loop that never ends is called an **infinite loop**. It usually happens when the condition never evaluates to `false`.

Example:

```
// Infinite loop (Avoid this in practice)
while (true) {
  console.log("This will run forever!");
}
```

To prevent infinite loops, ensure the loop's condition changes during execution.

Multiple-Choice Questions

What does this code output?

```
for (let i = 0; i < 3; i++) {
  console.log(i);
}
```

1. 0 1 2
2. 1 2 3
3. 0 1 2 3
4. undefined

Answer: 1. 0 1 2
Explanation: The loop initializes i to 0, checks the condition i < 3, and increments i after each iteration. The loop stops when i equals 3.

What is the main difference between while and do...while loops?

1. while executes the loop body once, do...while does not.
2. do...while always executes the loop body at least once.
3. while can only work with numbers.
4. do...while cannot use conditions.

Answer: 2. do...while always executes the loop body at least once.
Explanation: In a do...while loop, the body is executed first, then the condition is checked.

What will this code output?

```
let i = 0;
while (i < 3) {
  console.log(i);
  i++;
```

```
}
```

1. 0 1 2
2. 1 2 3
3. undefined
4. Infinite loop

Answer: 1. 0 1 2
Explanation: The loop initializes i to 0 and increments i after each iteration until i < 3 evaluates to false.

What is the output of this code?
```
let i = 5;
do {
  console.log(i);
  i--;
} while (i > 0);
```

1. 5 4 3 2 1
2. 4 3 2 1
3. 5 4 3 2 1 0
4. undefined

Answer: 1. 5 4 3 2 1
Explanation: The do...while loop decrements i until i > 0 is false.

What is the result of this code?
```
for (let i = 1; i <= 3; i++) {
  console.log(i * 2);
}
```

1. 2 4 6
2. 1 2 3
3. 6 4 2
4. undefined

Answer: 1. 2 4 6
Explanation: The loop multiplies i by 2 on each iteration and logs the result.

What does this code output?
```
for (let i = 0; i < 3; i++) {
  if (i === 1) continue;
  console.log(i);
}
```
   1. 0 1 2
   2. 0 2
   3. 0 1
   4. 2

Answer: 2. 0 2
Explanation: The continue statement skips the iteration when i === 1.

Which loop guarantees at least one execution of its body?
   1. for
   2. while
   3. do...while
   4. None of the above

Answer: 3. do...while
Explanation: The do...while loop executes the body before checking the condition.

What happens if the condition in a while loop is always true?
   1. The loop runs once.
   2. The loop runs forever.
   3. The loop runs twice.
   4. The loop does not run.

Answer: 2. The loop runs forever.
Explanation: If the condition is always `true`, the loop does not stop, resulting in an infinite loop.

What is the output of this code?
```
let i = 0;
while (i < 3) {
  console.log(i);
  i++;
}
```
1. 0 1 2
2. 1 2 3
3. Infinite loop
4. No output

Answer: 1. 0 1 2
Explanation: The loop starts at `i = 0` and increments `i` until the condition `i < 3` is false.

Which loop is most suitable when the number of iterations is known beforehand?
1. `for`
2. `while`
3. `do...while`
4. None of the above

Answer: 1. `for`
Explanation: The `for` loop is best suited for scenarios where the number of iterations is predefined.

What is the output of this code?
```
for (let i = 1; i <= 5; i++) {
  if (i === 3) break;
  console.log(i);
}
```

1. 1 2 3
2. 1 2
3. 1 2 3 4 5
4. No output

Answer: 2. 1 2
Explanation: The break statement stops the loop when i
=== 3.

What will this code output?

```
let count = 0;
do {
  console.log(count);
  count++;
} while (count < 3);
```

1. 0 1 2
2. 0 1
3. 1 2 3
4. No output

Answer: 1. 0 1 2
Explanation: The do...while loop runs the body at least
once and increments count until the condition count < 3
is false.

Which loop is most suitable for iterating over the
characters of a string?

1. for
2. while
3. do...while
4. All of the above

Answer: 4. All of the above
Explanation: All loop types can iterate over a string,
though for is typically more concise for this use case.

What is the output of this code?

```
for (let i = 10; i >= 8; i--) {
  console.log(i);
}
```

1. 10 9 8
2. 8 9 10
3. 10 9
4. Infinite loop

Answer: 1. 10 9 8

Explanation: The loop decrements i from 10 until i >= 8 is false.

What does this code output?

```
let x = 1;
while (x < 3) {
  console.log(x);
  x++;
}
```

1. 1 2
2. 1 2 3
3. 1
4. Infinite loop

Answer: 1. 1 2

Explanation: The loop increments x from 1 until x < 3 evaluates to false.

What is the result of this code?

```
for (let i = 0; i < 5; i += 2) {
  console.log(i);
}
```

1. 0 2 4

2. 1 3
3. 0 1 2 3 4
4. Infinite loop

Answer: 1. 0 2 4
Explanation: The loop increments i by 2 after each iteration until i < 5 evaluates to false.

What will this code output?

```
let n = 5;
while (n > 0) {
  n--;
  if (n === 2) continue;
  console.log(n);
}
```

1. 4 3 1 0
2. 4 3 2 1 0
3. 4 3 2 1
4. Infinite loop

Answer: 1. 4 3 1 0
Explanation: The continue statement skips the iteration when n === 2.

Which loop guarantees execution of the block at least once, even if the condition is false initially?

1. for
2. while
3. do...while
4. None

Answer: 3. do...while
Explanation: The do...while loop executes the body before checking the condition.

What is the output of this code?

```
let i = 0;
do {
    console.log(i);
} while (i > 0);
```

    1. 0
    2. No output
    3. Infinite loop
    4. `undefined`

Answer: 1. 0
Explanation: The `do...while` loop executes the block once before checking the condition, even though the condition is false.

What does this code output?

```
let sum = 0;
for (let i = 1; i <= 3; i++) {
    sum += i;
}
console.log(sum);
```

    1. 6
    2. 5
    3. 3
    4. 0

Answer: 1. 6
Explanation: The loop adds 1 + 2 + 3 to sum, resulting in 6.

What will happen if the condition in a while loop is always false?

    1. The loop executes once.
    2. The loop does not execute.

3. The loop runs infinitely.
4. An error occurs.

Answer: 2. The loop does not execute.
Explanation: The `while` loop checks the condition before running, so if it's `false`, the loop doesn't execute.

What does this code output?

```
for (let i = 0; i < 4; i++) {
  for (let j = 0; j < 2; j++) {
    console.log(`${i}, ${j}`);
  }
}
```

1. `(0, 0), (1, 0), (2, 0), (3, 0)`
2. `(0, 0), (0, 1), (1, 0), (1, 1), (2, 0), (2, 1), (3, 0), (3, 1)`
3. `(0, 1), (1, 2), (2, 3)`
4. Infinite loop

Answer: 2. `(0, 0), (0, 1), (1, 0), (1, 1), (2, 0), (2, 1), (3, 0), (3, 1)`
Explanation: The outer loop runs 4 times, and the inner loop runs 2 times for each iteration of the outer loop.

Which statement is true about the break statement?

1. It stops the loop immediately.
2. It skips the current iteration and continues.
3. It can only be used in `while` loops.
4. It causes an error if used in `for` loops.

Answer: 1. It stops the loop immediately.
Explanation: The `break` statement terminates the loop, regardless of the loop type.

What is the output of this code?

```
for (let i = 1; i <= 3; i++) {
```

```
for (let j = 1; j <= 2; j++) {
  if (j === 2) break;
  console.log(`${i}, ${j}`);
}
}
```

1. (1, 1), (2, 1), (3, 1)
2. (1, 1), (1, 2), (2, 1), (2, 2), (3, 1), (3, 2)
3. Infinite loop
4. No output

Answer: 1. (1, 1), (2, 1), (3, 1)

Explanation: The break exits the inner loop when j === 2, so only (i, 1) pairs are logged.

What is the result of this code?

```
let i = 3;
while (i--) {
  console.log(i);
}
```

1. 3 2 1
2. 2 1 0
3. 3 2 1 0
4. Infinite loop

Answer: 2. 2 1 0

Explanation: The i-- decrements i and evaluates the condition. The loop runs while i is greater than 0.

Iterating Over Arrays with forEach in JavaScript

1. What is forEach?

The `forEach` method is an array method in JavaScript that is used to iterate over each element in an array. It executes a provided function once for each array element.

2. Syntax of forEach

```
array.forEach(function(element, index,
array) {
    // Code to execute
});
```

Parameters:

1. **element**: The current element in the array.

2. **index**: The index of the current element (optional).

3. **array**: The array being iterated over (optional).

3. Basic Example

```
const fruits = ["apple", "banana",
"cherry"];
fruits.forEach(function(fruit) {
    console.log(fruit);
});
```

Output:

```
apple
banana
cherry
```

4. Using forEach with Arrow Functions

You can use arrow functions for a more concise syntax:

```
fruits.forEach((fruit) =>
console.log(fruit));
```

5. Accessing the Index

You can access the index of each element during iteration:

```
fruits.forEach((fruit, index) => {
    console.log(`${index}: ${fruit}`);
});
```

Output:

```
0: apple
1: banana
2: cherry
```

6. Modifying Elements

You cannot modify the array directly inside `forEach` because it does not return a value. For creating a new array with modified elements, use methods like map.

Incorrect Usage:

```
fruits.forEach((fruit) => {
    fruit = fruit.toUpperCase(); // Does not
modify the original array
});
console.log(fruits); // ["apple", "banana",
"cherry"]
```

7. Breaking Out of forEach

You cannot use `break` or `continue` within a `forEach` loop. To achieve similar behavior, use a `for` loop or some/every methods.

8. Practical Use Cases of forEach

1. Logging or printing elements.
2. Applying a function to each element.

3. Summing up numbers in an array.

Example: Summing Numbers:

```
const numbers = [1, 2, 3, 4, 5];
let sum = 0;
numbers.forEach((number) => {
  sum += number;
});
console.log(sum); // 15
```

Multiple-Choice Questions

What is the primary purpose of the forEach method?
1. To iterate over an array and execute a function for each element.
2. To modify the array elements directly.
3. To create a new array from an existing one.
4. To sort an array.

Answer: 1. To iterate over an array and execute a function for each element.

Explanation: The forEach method is designed to perform a specified action for each element in an array.

What does this code output?

```
const fruits = ["apple", "banana",
"cherry"];
fruits.forEach((fruit) =>
console.log(fruit));
```

1. ["apple", "banana", "cherry"]
2. apple banana cherry
3. banana cherry apple
4. No output

Answer: 2. `apple banana cherry`
Explanation: The `forEach` method logs each element in the order they appear in the array.

Which parameters can the callback function of forEach accept?
1. `element, index, array`
2. `index, array, element`
3. `array, index, element`
4. None

Answer: 1. `element, index, array`
Explanation: The callback function receives the current element, its index, and the array being iterated over.

What is the result of this code?
```
const numbers = [1, 2, 3];
numbers.forEach((number) => {
  number = number * 2;
});
console.log(numbers);
```
1. `[2, 4, 6]`
2. `[1, 2, 3]`
3. `[undefined, undefined, undefined]`
4. Error

Answer: 2. `[1, 2, 3]`
Explanation: The `forEach` method does not modify the original array; it executes the callback on each element independently.

Can you return a value from forEach to create a new array?
1. Yes
2. No

Answer: 2. No
Explanation: The forEach method does not return a new array. Use map to create a new array.

What is the output of this code?
```
const letters = ["a", "b", "c"];
letters.forEach((letter, index) => {
  console.log(`${index}: ${letter}`);
});
```
    1. 0: a 1: b 2: c
    2. a: 0 b: 1 c: 2
    3. ["a", "b", "c"]
    4. Error

Answer: 1. 0: a 1: b 2: c
Explanation: The second parameter of forEach is the index of the current element.

Which of the following is true about forEach?
    1. It can break out of the loop.
    2. It skips undefined elements.
    3. It is asynchronous.
    4. It cannot use break or continue.

Answer: 4. It cannot use break or continue.
Explanation: The forEach method does not allow breaking or skipping iterations. Use a for loop if this behavior is required.

What will this code output?
```
const arr = [1, 2, 3];
arr.forEach((num) => {
  console.log(num * 2);
});
```
    1. 2 4 6

2. `[2, 4, 6]`
3. `[1, 2, 3]`
4. Error

Answer: 1. 2 4 6
Explanation: The callback multiplies each element by 2 and logs the result.

What happens if forEach is called on an empty array?
1. It throws an error.
2. It executes the callback function once.
3. It does nothing.
4. It skips the first element.

Answer: 3. It does nothing.
Explanation: The forEach method does not execute the callback for empty arrays.

What is the output of this code?
```
const nums = [1, 2, 3];
nums.forEach((num, index) => {
  nums[index] = num * 2;
});
console.log(nums);
```
1. `[1, 2, 3]`
2. `[2, 4, 6]`
3. undefined
4. Error

Answer: 2. `[2, 4, 6]`
Explanation: The callback modifies the original array directly by updating each element.

What does this code output?
```
const colors = ["red", "green", "blue"];
colors.forEach((color) => {
```

```
  console.log(color.toUpperCase());
});
```
1. RED GREEN BLUE
2. [RED, GREEN, BLUE]
3. [red, green, blue]
4. Error

Answer: 1. RED GREEN BLUE
Explanation: The toUpperCase method converts each string element to uppercase, and forEach logs each modified string.

What is the result of this code?
```
const names = ["Alice", "Bob", "Charlie"];
names.forEach((name, index, array) => {
  console.log(array[index]);
});
```
1. Alice Bob Charlie
2. [Alice, Bob, Charlie]
3. undefined
4. Error

Answer: 1. Alice Bob Charlie
Explanation: The array parameter references the original array, and array[index] accesses each element.

What happens when you use return inside a forEach callback?
1. It stops the loop.
2. It skips the current iteration.
3. It returns a value from the callback but doesn't affect the loop.
4. It throws an error.

Answer: 3. It returns a value from the callback but doesn't affect the loop.

Explanation: The `return` statement inside a `forEach` callback only affects the callback function and does not stop or skip iterations.

What is the output of this code?
```
const arr = [10, 20, 30];
arr.forEach((num) => {
    if (num > 15) console.log(num);
});
```
1. 20 30
2. 10 20 30
3. [20, 30]
4. No output

Answer: 1. 20 30
Explanation: The callback logs numbers greater than 15, so only 20 and 30 are printed.

Which statement about forEach is correct?
1. It is asynchronous.
2. It modifies the array by default.
3. It iterates over all elements, including empty slots.
4. It skips empty slots in sparse arrays.

Answer: 4. It skips empty slots in sparse arrays.
Explanation: The `forEach` method skips empty slots but processes all defined elements.

What does this code output?
```
const nums = [1, 2, 3];
let result = 0;
nums.forEach((num) => {
    result += num;
});
console.log(result);
```

1. 6
2. [1, 2, 3]
3. 123
4. Error

Answer: 1. 6
Explanation: The callback adds each element to `result`, producing the sum 1 + 2 + 3 = 6.

What will this code output?
```
const animals = ["cat", "dog", "bird"];
animals.forEach((animal, index) => {
  console.log(`${index + 1}: ${animal}`);
});
```
1. 1: cat 2: dog 3: bird
2. 0: cat 1: dog 2: bird
3. [cat, dog, bird]
4. No output

Answer: 1. 1: cat 2: dog 3: bird
Explanation: The callback uses `index + 1` to create a 1-based index for each element.

What happens if you try to break out of a forEach loop using break?
1. It stops the loop.
2. It skips the current iteration.
3. It throws an error.
4. It continues to the next iteration.

Answer: 3. It throws an error.
Explanation: The `forEach` method does not support `break` or `continue`. Use a `for` loop if this behavior is required.

What does this code output?
```
const items = ["a", "b", "c"];
items.forEach((item) => {
  console.log(item.repeat(2));
});
```
    1. aa bb cc
    2. [aa, bb, cc]
    3. Error
    4. No output

Answer: 1. aa bb cc
Explanation: The repeat method repeats each string twice, and forEach logs the result.

What is the output of this code?
```
const arr = [5, 10, 15];
arr.forEach((num, index) => {
  console.log(num + index);
});
```
    1. 5 11 17
    2. 5 10 15
    3. 6 12 18
    4. Error

Answer: 1. 5 11 17
Explanation: The callback adds the current element (num) and its index (index) and logs the result.

Which of the following is NOT true about forEach?
    1. It can be used to modify the original array.
    2. It is asynchronous.
    3. It cannot be stopped with break.
    4. It skips empty slots in arrays.

Answer: 2. It is asynchronous.
Explanation: The forEach method is synchronous and processes one element at a time.

What does this code output?
```
const arr = [2, 4, 6];
arr.forEach((num) => {
  if (num % 2 === 0) console.log("Even");
});
```
1. Even Even Even
2. Even Even
3. No output
4. Error

Answer: 1. Even Even Even
Explanation: All elements in the array are even, so the callback logs "Even" for each element.

What will this code output?
```
const cities = ["Paris", "London", "New York"];
cities.forEach((city) => {
  if (city === "London") {
    console.log("Found London");
  }
});
```
1. Found London
2. Paris Found London New York
3. No output
4. Error

Answer: 1. Found London
Explanation: The callback logs "Found London" only when the element equals "London".

What happens if you modify an array inside forEach?
1. The changes affect subsequent iterations.
2. The array is unchanged.
3. It throws an error.
4. Only the modified elements are processed.

Answer: 1. The changes affect subsequent iterations.
Explanation: Modifying the array during iteration affects subsequent elements.

What does this code output?
```
const numbers = [1, 2, 3];
numbers.forEach((num, index, array) => {
  array[index] = num * 2;
});
console.log(numbers);
```
1. [1, 2, 3]
2. [2, 4, 6]
3. undefined
4. Error

Answer: 2. [2, 4, 6]
Explanation: The callback modifies the original array directly, multiplying each element by 2.

Parameters and Return Values in JavaScript

1. Function Parameters
Parameters are placeholders in a function definition that allow you to pass data into the function when it is called.
Syntax:
```
function greet(name) {
  console.log(`Hello, ${name}!`);
```

```
}
greet("Alice"); // Outputs: Hello, Alice!
```

- **Parameters**: name is the parameter in the function definition.
- **Arguments**: "Alice" is the argument passed to the function.

2. Multiple Parameters

Functions can take multiple parameters, separated by commas.

```
function add(a, b) {
   return a + b;
}
console.log(add(5, 3)); // Outputs: 8
```

3. Default Parameters

You can assign default values to parameters. If no argument is passed, the parameter takes the default value.

```
function greet(name = "Guest") {
   console.log(`Hello, ${name}!`);
}
greet(); // Outputs: Hello, Guest!
```

4. Rest Parameters

The rest parameter syntax (...) allows a function to accept an indefinite number of arguments as an array.

```
function sum(...numbers) {
   return numbers.reduce((total, num) =>
total + num, 0);
}
console.log(sum(1, 2, 3, 4)); // Outputs:
10
```

5. Return Values

Functions can return values using the `return` statement. The returned value can be assigned to a variable or used directly.

```
function square(num) {
    return num * num;
}
console.log(square(4)); // Outputs: 16
```

If a function does not have a `return` statement, it returns `undefined` by default.

6. Returning Objects

Functions can return any type of value, including objects.

```
function createUser(name, age) {
    return { name, age };
}
console.log(createUser("Alice", 30)); //
Outputs: { name: "Alice", age: 30 }
```

7. Combining Parameters and Return Values

Parameters allow functions to accept data, while return values allow them to produce results. Together, they enable reusable and modular code.

```
function calculateArea(length, width) {
    return length * width;
}
console.log(calculateArea(5, 10)); //
Outputs: 50
```

Multiple-Choice Questions

What is the primary purpose of parameters in a function?

1. To return values from a function.
2. To accept input values when the function is called.
3. To define a function without executing it.
4. To loop through an array.

Answer: 2. To accept input values when the function is called.

Explanation: Parameters act as placeholders for values that are passed into the function during execution.

What does this code output?

```
function greet(name) {
  console.log(`Hello, ${name}!`);
}
greet("John");
```

1. `Hello, name!`
2. `Hello, John!`
3. `Hello, undefined!`
4. `undefined`

Answer: 2. `Hello, John!`

Explanation: The argument "John" is passed to the name parameter, and the function outputs the formatted string.

What is the output of this code?

```
function add(a, b = 5) {
  return a + b;
}
console.log(add(10));
```

1. `15`
2. `10`

3. 5

4. `undefined`

Answer: 1. 15

Explanation: The second parameter, b, has a default value of 5. When the function is called with one argument, b takes its default value.

What will this code output?
```
function multiply(a, b) {
    return a * b;
}
console.log(multiply(4));
```
1. 16

2. NaN

3. 4

4. `undefined`

Answer: 2. NaN

Explanation: The second parameter, b, is `undefined` because no argument is passed, and 4 * `undefined` evaluates to NaN.

What does the return statement do in a function?
1. Ends the function execution and returns a value.
2. Skips the current iteration of a loop.
3. Repeats the function execution.
4. Declares a variable inside the function.

Answer: 1. Ends the function execution and returns a value.

Explanation: The `return` statement stops the function's execution and specifies a value to be returned.

What will this code output?
```
function sayHello() {
```

```
    return "Hello, World!";
}
console.log(sayHello());
```
1. "Hello, World!"
2. undefined
3. Error
4. No output

Answer: 1. "Hello, World!"
Explanation: The function returns the string "Hello, World!", which is logged to the console.

What does this code output?
```
function add(...numbers) {
   return numbers.reduce((sum, num) => sum +
num, 0);
}
console.log(add(1, 2, 3, 4));
```
1. 10
2. 1234
3. [1, 2, 3, 4]
4. undefined

Answer: 1. 10
Explanation: The rest parameter ...numbers collects all arguments into an array. The reduce method sums up the elements, resulting in 10.

What happens if a function does not have a return statement?
1. It returns null.
2. It throws an error.
3. It returns undefined.
4. It always returns 0.

Answer: 3. It returns undefined.
Explanation: If a function has no `return` statement, it implicitly returns undefined.

What is the output of this code?

```
function square(num) {
    return num * num;
}
console.log(square(4));
```
    1. 16
    2. 4
    3. 8
    4. undefined

Answer: 1. 16
Explanation: The function multiplies the input num by itself and returns the result.

What is the output of this code?

```
function subtract(a, b = 10) {
    return a - b;
}
console.log(subtract(30, 20));
```
    1. 10
    2. 20
    3. 30
    4. undefined

Answer: 1. 10
Explanation: The argument 20 overrides the default value of b. The function returns 30 - 20 = 10.

What is the output of this code?

```
function greet(name = "Guest") {
```

```
    return `Hello, ${name}!`;
}
console.log(greet());
```
1. `Hello, !`
2. `Hello, Guest!`
3. `Hello, undefined!`
4. `Error`

Answer: 2. `Hello, Guest!`
Explanation: The default value "`Guest`" is used for the name parameter since no argument is provided.

What happens if you pass more arguments than there are parameters?
```
function add(a, b) {
    return a + b;
}
console.log(add(1, 2, 3));
```
1. It throws an error.
2. It ignores extra arguments.
3. It adds all the arguments.
4. It returns `undefined`.

Answer: 2. It ignores extra arguments.
Explanation: JavaScript functions only consider the defined parameters. Extra arguments are ignored unless handled using `arguments` or rest parameters.

What is the output of this code?
```
function calculateArea(length, width = 10)
{
    return length * width;
}
console.log(calculateArea(5));
```

1. 50
2. 5
3. undefined
4. Error

Answer: 1. 50
Explanation: The default value of width is used, so the function calculates 5 * 10.

What does this code output?
```
function multiply(a, b) {
  console.log(a * b);
}
console.log(multiply(2, 3));
```
1. 6
2. 6 undefined
3. undefined
4. Error

Answer: 2. 6 undefined
Explanation: The function logs 6 but does not have a return statement, so it implicitly returns undefined.

What is the output of this code?
```
function createUser(name, age) {
  return { name, age };
}
console.log(createUser("Alice", 30));
```
1. { name: "Alice", age: 30 }
2. Alice 30
3. [Alice, 30]
4. undefined

Answer: 1. `{ name: "Alice", age: 30 }`
Explanation: The function returns an object with name and age properties.

What does this code output?

```
function sum(...nums) {
  return nums.length;
}
console.log(sum(1, 2, 3, 4));
```

1. 4
2. [1, 2, 3, 4]
3. 10
4. undefined

Answer: 1. 4
Explanation: The rest parameter `...nums` collects all arguments into an array. The `length` property of the array is 4.

What is the purpose of default parameters in functions?

1. To make all parameters required.
2. To provide fallback values for parameters when arguments are not passed.
3. To return a default value if the function is not called.
4. To prevent the function from executing.

Answer: 2. To provide fallback values for parameters when arguments are not passed.
Explanation: Default parameters allow a function to use a specified value when no argument is provided.

What happens when a function returns an object using the return statement?

```
function getUser(name, age) {
  return { name: name, age: age };
```

```
}
console.log(getUser("John", 25));
```
1. undefined
2. { name: "John", age: 25 }
3. Error
4. No output

Answer: 2. { name: "John", age: 25 }
Explanation: The function returns an object with name and age properties initialized using the arguments.

What is the output of this code?
```
function subtract(a, b = 10) {
  return a - b;
}
console.log(subtract(20));
```
1. 10
2. 20
3. undefined
4. Error

Answer: 1. 10
Explanation: The default value of b is 10, so the function returns 20 - 10 = 10.

What will this code output?
```
function multiply(a, b) {
  return a * b;
}
console.log(multiply(2));
```
1. 4
2. NaN
3. 2

4. undefined

Answer: 2. NaN

Explanation: The second parameter b is undefined since no argument is passed, and 2 * undefined results in NaN.

What is the output of this code?

```
function getName(name = "Anonymous") {
  return name;
}
console.log(getName());
```

1. Anonymous
2. undefined
3. Error
4. null

Answer: 1. Anonymous

Explanation: The default value "Anonymous" is used since no argument is provided.

What does this code output?

```
function greet(name, age) {
  console.log(`Hello, ${name}. You are
${age} years old.`);
}
greet("Alice");
```

1. Hello, Alice. You are undefined years old.
2. Hello, Alice. You are years old.
3. Error
4. No output

Answer: 1. Hello, Alice. You are undefined years old.

Explanation: The second parameter age is undefined because no argument is provided for it.

What is the output of this code?

```
function square(num) {
   return num ** 2;
}
console.log(square(3));
```

    1. 9

    2. 6

    3. 3

    4. undefined

Answer: 1. 9

Explanation: The function raises num to the power of 2 using the exponentiation operator (**).

What happens if a return statement is missing in a function?

    1. It returns null.

    2. It returns undefined.

    3. It throws an error.

    4. It does not execute.

Answer: 2. It returns undefined.

Explanation: If a return statement is absent, the function implicitly returns undefined.

What does this code output?

```
function calculate(a, b) {
   return {
     sum: a + b,
     product: a * b
   };
```

```
}
console.log(calculate(3, 4));
```
1. `{ sum: 7, product: 12 }`
2. `{ sum: "34", product: "12" }`
3. `[7, 12]`
4. `undefined`

Answer: 1. `{ sum: 7, product: 12 }`
Explanation: The function returns an object with properties sum and `product`, calculated using the arguments.

Creating and Manipulating Objects in JavaScript

Objects are a fundamental part of JavaScript and are used to store data in key-value pairs. They can represent real-world entities, such as a person, car, or product.

1. Creating an Object

An object can be created using object literal syntax, the `Object` constructor, or `class`.

Object Literal:
```
const person = {
  name: "Alice",
  age: 30,
  greet: function() {
    console.log("Hello!");
  },
};
```
Using the `Object` Constructor:
```
const car = new Object();
car.brand = "Toyota";
car.model = "Corolla";
```

Using a Class:

```
class Person {
  constructor(name, age) {
    this.name = name;
    this.age = age;
  }
}
const person1 = new Person("Alice", 30);
```

2. Accessing Object Properties

Properties can be accessed using dot notation or bracket notation.

Dot Notation:

```
console.log(person.name); // Outputs: Alice
```

Bracket Notation:

```
console.log(person["age"]); // Outputs: 30
```

3. Adding and Modifying Properties

You can add or modify properties directly.

```
person.city = "New York"; // Adding a new
property
person.age = 31;          // Modifying an
existing property
```

4. Deleting Properties

Use the delete operator to remove a property.

```
delete person.city;
console.log(person.city); // Outputs:
undefined
```

5. Iterating Over an Object

Use a for...in loop to iterate over all enumerable properties.

```
for (let key in person) {
  console.log(`${key}: ${person[key]}`);
}
```

6. Checking for Property Existence

Use the in operator or hasOwnProperty method.

```
console.log("name" in person);          //
Outputs: true
console.log(person.hasOwnProperty("age"));
// Outputs: true
```

7. Object Methods

Objects can have methods (functions as properties).

```
const calculator = {
  add(a, b) {
    return a + b;
  },
};
console.log(calculator.add(5, 3)); //
Outputs: 8
```

8. Object.keys(), Object.values(), and Object.entries()

These methods are used to retrieve keys, values, and entries from an object.

```
console.log(Object.keys(person));     //
Outputs: ["name", "age"]
console.log(Object.values(person)); //
Outputs: ["Alice", 30]
console.log(Object.entries(person)); //
Outputs: [["name", "Alice"], ["age", 30]]
```

9. Copying Objects

Use `Object.assign()` or the spread operator (`...`) to copy an object.

```
const copy = { ...person }; // Shallow copy
```

Multiple-Choice Questions

How do you create an object using object literal syntax?

1. `let obj = {};`
2. `let obj = new Object();`
3. `let obj = Object.create();`
4. `let obj = Object();`

Answer: 1. `let obj = {};`
Explanation: Object literal syntax uses curly braces {} to define an object.

How do you add a property to an object?

1. `obj.property = value;`
2. `obj["property"] = value;`
3. Both 1 and 2
4. You cannot add properties to an object dynamically.

Answer: 3. Both 1 and 2
Explanation: Properties can be added using dot notation or bracket notation.

What will this code output?

```
const obj = { a: 1, b: 2 };
delete obj.a;
console.log(obj);
```

1. `{}`
2. `{ a: 1, b: 2 }`
3. `{ b: 2 }`

4. undefined

Answer: 3. `{ b: 2 }`
Explanation: The `delete` operator removes the a property from the object.

What does this code output?

```
const obj = { a: 1, b: 2 };
console.log("a" in obj);
```
1. true
2. false
3. undefined
4. Error

Answer: 1. true
Explanation: The `in` operator checks if the property a exists in the object.

What will this code output?

```
const person = { name: "Alice", age: 30 };
console.log(Object.keys(person));
```
1. `["name", "age"]`
2. `["Alice", 30]`
3. Error
4. undefined

Answer: 1. `["name", "age"]`
Explanation: The `Object.keys()` method returns an array of the object's keys.

What is the output of this code?

```
const person = { name: "Bob", greet() {
return "Hello!"; } };
console.log(person.greet());
```
1. `"Hello!"`

2. `undefined`
3. `Error`
4. `null`

Answer: 1. `"Hello!"`
Explanation: The `greet` method is a function in the object and returns `"Hello!"`.

What happens when you use Object.assign()?
1. It creates a deep copy of an object.
2. It merges properties from source objects into a target object.
3. It deletes properties from an object.
4. It creates a new object from a class.

Answer: 2. It merges properties from source objects into a target object.
Explanation: `Object.assign()` copies properties from one or more source objects to a target object.

How can you check if a property exists in an object?
1. `obj.hasOwnProperty("property");`
2. `"property" in obj;`
3. Both 1 and 2
4. `obj.propertyExists();`

Answer: 3. Both 1 and 2
Explanation: Both `hasOwnProperty` and the `in` operator check for property existence.

What does this code output?
```
const car = { brand: "Toyota", model:
"Corolla" };
console.log(Object.values(car));
```
1. `["Toyota", "Corolla"]`
2. `["brand", "model"]`
3. `Error`

4. undefined

Answer: 1. `["Toyota", "Corolla"]`
Explanation: The `Object.values()` method returns an array of the object's values.

What does this code output?
```
const obj = { a: 1, b: 2 };
for (let key in obj) {
  console.log(key);
}
```
    1. a b
    2. 1 2
    3. Error
    4. undefined

Answer: 1. a b
Explanation: The `for...in` loop iterates over the object's keys.

What will this code output?
```
const user = { name: "Alice", age: 25 };
user.age = 30;
console.log(user);
```
    1. `{ name: "Alice", age: 30 }`
    2. `{ name: "Alice", age: 25 }`
    3. undefined
    4. Error

Answer: 1. `{ name: "Alice", age: 30 }`
Explanation: You can modify an object's properties, even if the object is declared with `const`.

What is the output of this code?
```
const obj = { a: 1, b: 2 };
```

```
console.log(obj.c);
```
1. null
2. undefined
3. Error
4. {}

Answer: 2. undefined
Explanation: Accessing a property that doesn't exist on an object returns undefined.

How can you copy an object in JavaScript?
1. `Object.assign({}, obj);`
2. `{ ...obj };`
3. Both 1 and 2
4. `copy(obj);`

Answer: 3. Both 1 and 2
Explanation: Both Object.assign and the spread operator create shallow copies of objects.

What will this code output?
```
const obj = { a: 1 };
Object.freeze(obj);
obj.a = 2;
console.log(obj.a);
```
1. 1
2. 2
3. undefined
4. Error

Answer: 1. 1
Explanation: The Object.freeze method prevents modification of existing properties.

What does this code output?

```
const user = { name: "John", age: 25 };
console.log(Object.entries(user));
```

1. [["John", 25]]
2. ["name", "John", "age", 25]
3. [["name", "John"], ["age", 25]]
4. undefined

Answer: 3. [["name", "John"], ["age", 25]]
Explanation: The Object.entries method returns an array of key-value pairs as subarrays.

What is the output of this code?

```
const obj = { a: 1, b: 2 };
console.log(obj.hasOwnProperty("c"));
```

1. true
2. false
3. undefined
4. Error

Answer: 2. false
Explanation: The hasOwnProperty method checks if the object directly contains the specified property.

What will this code output?

```
const obj = { a: 1, b: { c: 2 } };
const copy = { ...obj };
copy.b.c = 3;
console.log(obj.b.c);
```

1. 2
2. 3
3. undefined
4. Error

Answer: 2. 3
Explanation: The spread operator creates a shallow copy, so nested objects remain linked to the original.

What is the purpose of Object.seal?
1. To prevent adding or removing properties.
2. To prevent modifying property values.
3. To prevent reading the properties.
4. To create a deep copy of the object.

Answer: 1. To prevent adding or removing properties.
Explanation: Object.seal allows modifying existing properties but disallows adding or deleting properties.

What will this code output?
```
const person = { name: "Alice" };
person.name = "Bob";
console.log(person.name);
```
1. "Alice"
2. "Bob"
3. undefined
4. Error

Answer: 2. "Bob"
Explanation: Objects declared with const can have their properties modified.

What is the output of this code?
```
const car = { brand: "Toyota" };
car.model = "Corolla";
console.log(car);
```
1. { brand: "Toyota" }
2. { brand: "Toyota", model: "Corolla" }
3. undefined
4. Error

Answer: 2. `{ brand: "Toyota", model: "Corolla" }`

Explanation: You can add new properties to an object dynamically.

Which statement about Object.assign() is correct?

1. It creates a deep copy of the object.
2. It copies properties from one or more source objects to a target object.
3. It prevents modification of properties.
4. It creates a prototype chain.

Answer: 2. It copies properties from one or more source objects to a target object.

Explanation: `Object.assign` performs a shallow copy and merges properties into the target object.

What will this code output?

```
const obj = { a: 1, b: 2 };
Object.defineProperty(obj, "c", { value: 3
});
console.log(obj.c);
```

1. `3`
2. `undefined`
3. `Error`
4. `{ a: 1, b: 2, c: 3 }`

Answer: 1. 3

Explanation: `Object.defineProperty` adds a non-enumerable property c to the object.

What is the output of this code?

```
const person = { name: "Alice", age: 30 };
delete person.age;
console.log(person);
```

1. `{ name: "Alice" }`

2. `{ name: "Alice", age: 30 }`

3. `undefined`

4. `Error`

Answer: 1. `{ name: "Alice" }`
Explanation: The `delete` operator removes the `age` property from the object.

Which method can you use to get all the enumerable property names of an object?

1. `Object.keys()`

2. `Object.values()`

3. `Object.entries()`

4. `Object.getOwnPropertyNames()`

Answer: 1. `Object.keys()`
Explanation: `Object.keys()` returns an array of enumerable property names of the object.

What is the output of this code?
```
const obj = { a: 1, b: 2 };
console.log(obj["a"]);
```

1. `1`

2. `"a"`

3. `undefined`

4. `Error`

Answer: 1. `1`
Explanation: Bracket notation accesses the value of the property a, which is 1.

Common Array Methods in JavaScript

JavaScript arrays are versatile and come with numerous built-in methods to perform common tasks such as adding, removing, transforming, and filtering elements.

1. Adding and Removing Elements

push: Adds one or more elements to the end of the array and returns the new length.

```
const fruits = ["apple", "banana"];
fruits.push("cherry");
console.log(fruits); // Outputs: ["apple", "banana", "cherry"]
```

pop: Removes the last element from the array and returns it.

```
const lastFruit = fruits.pop();
console.log(lastFruit); // Outputs: "cherry"
```

unshift: Adds one or more elements to the beginning of the array.

```
fruits.unshift("orange");
console.log(fruits); // Outputs: ["orange", "apple", "banana"]
```

shift: Removes the first element from the array and returns it.

```
const firstFruit = fruits.shift();
console.log(firstFruit); // Outputs: "orange"
```

2. Iterating Over Arrays

forEach: Executes a provided function once for each array element.

```
fruits.forEach((fruit) =>
console.log(fruit));
```

map: Creates a new array by applying a function to each element.

```
const lengths = fruits.map((fruit) =>
fruit.length);
console.log(lengths); // Outputs: [5, 6]
```

3. Filtering Arrays

filter: Creates a new array with elements that satisfy a condition.

```
const longFruits = fruits.filter((fruit) =>
fruit.length > 5);
console.log(longFruits); // Outputs:
["banana"]
```

4. Searching and Finding

indexOf: Returns the first index of a specified element, or -1 if not found.

```
console.log(fruits.indexOf("apple")); //
Outputs: 0
```

find: Returns the first element that satisfies a condition.

```
const fruit = fruits.find((fruit) =>
fruit.startsWith("b"));
console.log(fruit); // Outputs: "banana"
```

includes: Checks if an array contains a specific element.

```
console.log(fruits.includes("cherry")); //
Outputs: false
```

5. Transforming Arrays

reduce: Reduces the array to a single value.

```
const totalLength = fruits.reduce((sum,
fruit) => sum + fruit.length, 0);
console.log(totalLength); // Outputs: 11
```

6. Sorting Arrays

sort: Sorts the elements of an array in place.

```
fruits.sort();
console.log(fruits); // Outputs: ["apple",
"banana"]
```

reverse: Reverses the order of the elements in an array.

```
fruits.reverse();
console.log(fruits); // Outputs: ["banana",
"apple"]
```

7. Slicing and Splicing

slice: Returns a shallow copy of a portion of an array.

```
const someFruits = fruits.slice(0, 1);
console.log(someFruits); // Outputs:
["banana"]
```

splice: Adds or removes elements from an array.

```
fruits.splice(1, 0, "cherry");
console.log(fruits); // Outputs: ["banana",
"cherry", "apple"]
```

Multiple-Choice Questions

What does the push method do?

1. Removes the last element from an array.
2. Adds one or more elements to the end of an array.
3. Adds one or more elements to the beginning of an array.
4. Creates a new array by transforming each element.

Answer: 2. Adds one or more elements to the end of an array.

Explanation: The push method appends elements to the end and returns the new length of the array.

What will this code output?

```
const nums = [1, 2, 3];
nums.pop();
console.log(nums);
```

1. `[1, 2]`
2. `[1, 2, 3]`
3. `[2, 3]`
4. `Error`

Answer: 1. `[1, 2]`
Explanation: The pop method removes the last element (3) from the array.

Which method creates a new array by applying a function to each element?

1. `forEach`
2. `map`
3. `filter`
4. `reduce`

Answer: 2. map
Explanation: The map method transforms each element and returns a new array.

What does this code output?

```
const words = ["one", "two", "three"];
const result = words.map((word) =>
word.length);
console.log(result);
```

1. `[3, 3, 5]`
2. `[3, 3, 3]`
3. `["one", "two", "three"]`
4. `Error`

Answer: 1. `[3, 3, 5]`
Explanation: The map method creates a new array with the lengths of each string.

Which method filters elements based on a condition?
1. map
2. filter
3. reduce
4. sort

Answer: 2. `filter`
Explanation: The `filter` method returns a new array containing elements that satisfy the condition.

What does this code output?
```
const nums = [1, 2, 3, 4];
const evenNums = nums.filter((num) => num %
2 === 0);
console.log(evenNums);
```
1. `[1, 3]`
2. `[2, 4]`
3. `[1, 2, 3, 4]`
4. `Error`

Answer: 2. `[2, 4]`
Explanation: The `filter` method returns elements that are divisible by 2.

What is the difference between forEach and map?
1. `forEach` creates a new array; map modifies the original array.
2. `forEach` modifies the array; map creates a new array.
3. `forEach` doesn't return a value; map returns a new array.

4. Both create new arrays.

Answer: 3. `forEach` doesn't return a value; `map` returns a new array.

Explanation: The `forEach` method performs an action for each element, while `map` creates a transformed array.

What does this code output?
```
const nums = [1, 2, 3, 4];
const sum = nums.reduce((total, num) =>
total + num, 0);
console.log(sum);
```
1. 10
2. [1, 2, 3, 4]
3. 0
4. Error

Answer: 1. 10
Explanation: The `reduce` method accumulates values (1 + 2 + 3 + 4 = 10).

Which method checks if an array includes a specific element?
1. `find`
2. `includes`
3. `filter`
4. `indexOf`

Answer: 2. `includes`
Explanation: The `includes` method checks for the existence of an element in an array.

What does this code output?
```
const fruits = ["apple", "banana",
"cherry"];
console.log(fruits.indexOf("banana"));
```

1. 1
2. 0
3. 2
4. -1

Answer: 1. 1
Explanation: The indexOf method returns the position of the first occurrence of "banana".

What does this code output?
```
const fruits = ["apple", "banana",
"cherry"];
console.log(fruits.slice(1, 3));
```
1. ["apple", "banana"]
2. ["banana", "cherry"]
3. ["cherry"]
4. Error

Answer: 2. ["banana", "cherry"]
Explanation: The slice method returns a shallow copy of the array starting from index 1 (inclusive) to index 3 (exclusive).

What will this code output?
```
const fruits = ["apple", "banana",
"cherry"];
fruits.splice(1, 1, "orange");
console.log(fruits);
```
1. ["apple", "orange", "cherry"]
2. ["apple", "cherry"]
3. ["apple", "banana", "orange",
   "cherry"]
4. Error

Answer: 1. `["apple", "orange", "cherry"]`
Explanation: The `splice` method removes 1 element at index 1 and inserts `"orange"` in its place.

Which method returns a reversed array?
1. `reverse`
2. `sort`
3. `reduce`
4. `filter`

Answer: 1. `reverse`
Explanation: The `reverse` method reverses the order of elements in an array in place.

What does this code output?
```
const nums = [3, 1, 4, 2];
nums.sort();
console.log(nums);
```
1. `[1, 2, 3, 4]`
2. `[3, 1, 4, 2]`
3. `[4, 3, 2, 1]`
4. `[1, 2, 3, 4]` but as strings

Answer: 4. `[1, 2, 3, 4]` but as strings
Explanation: The `sort` method converts elements to strings before comparing, so the array is sorted lexicographically.

What does this code output?
```
const nums = [1, 2, 3];
nums.unshift(0);
console.log(nums);
```
1. `[1, 2, 3, 0]`
2. `[0, 1, 2, 3]`

3. `[1, 2, 3]`

4. `Error`

Answer: 2. `[0, 1, 2, 3]`

Explanation: The unshift method adds elements to the beginning of the array.

What does this code output?

```
const nums = [1, 2, 3, 4];
const result = nums.find((num) => num > 2);
console.log(result);
```

1. `[3, 4]`

2. `3`

3. `4`

4. `undefined`

Answer: 2. 3

Explanation: The find method returns the first element that satisfies the condition (num > 2).

Which method can you use to check if any elements in an array satisfy a condition?

1. `every`

2. `some`

3. `find`

4. `filter`

Answer: 2. some

Explanation: The some method returns true if at least one element satisfies the condition.

What will this code output?

```
const nums = [1, 2, 3];
const allPositive = nums.every((num) => num
> 0);
```

```
console.log(allPositive);
```
    1. true
    2. false
    3. undefined
    4. Error

Answer: 1. true
Explanation: The every method checks if all elements satisfy the condition (num > 0).

What does this code output?
```
const nums = [1, 2, 3, 4];
console.log(nums.includes(3));
```
    1. true
    2. false
    3. undefined
    4. Error

Answer: 1. true
Explanation: The includes method checks if 3 is present in the array and returns true.

What does this code output?
```
const nums = [1, 2, 3];
nums.shift();
console.log(nums);
```
    1. [2, 3]
    2. [1, 2, 3]
    3. [3]
    4. Error

Answer: 1. [2, 3]
Explanation: The shift method removes the first element (1) from the array.

What will this code output?

```
const nums = [1, 2, 3, 4];
const result = nums.reduce((sum, num) =>
sum + num, 0);
console.log(result);
```

    1. 10
    2. [1, 2, 3, 4]
    3. 0
    4. undefined

Answer: 1. 10
Explanation: The reduce method sums up the elements
(1 + 2 + 3 + 4 = 10).

What does this code output?

```
const nums = [1, 2, 3];
nums.reverse();
console.log(nums);
```

    1. [1, 2, 3]
    2. [3, 2, 1]
    3. Error
    4. undefined

Answer: 2. [3, 2, 1]
Explanation: The reverse method reverses the order of
elements in place.

What does this code output?

```
const nums = [10, 20, 30];
const newNums = nums.map((num) => num /
10);
console.log(newNums);
```

    1. [1, 2, 3]
    2. [10, 20, 30]

3. `[0.1, 0.2, 0.3]`
4. `Error`

Answer: 1. `[1, 2, 3]`
Explanation: The map method divides each element by 10 and creates a new array.

What does this code output?
```
const fruits = ["apple", "banana",
"cherry"];
console.log(fruits.join(", "));
```
1. `apple, banana, cherry`
2. `["apple", "banana", "cherry"]`
3. `Error`
4. `undefined`

Answer: 1. `apple, banana, cherry`
Explanation: The `join` method concatenates array elements into a string, separated by `", "`.

What is the output of this code?
```
const nums = [1, 2, 3];
nums.fill(0);
console.log(nums);
```
1. `[1, 2, 3]`
2. `[0, 0, 0]`
3. `[0, 2, 3]`
4. `Error`

Answer: 2. `[0, 0, 0]`
Explanation: The `fill` method replaces all elements in the array with 0.

Selecting Elements in JavaScript (getElementById, querySelector, and more)

Selecting elements from the DOM (Document Object Model) is a fundamental part of working with JavaScript for web development. The DOM represents the structure of a web page, and JavaScript provides methods to interact with its elements.

1. Selecting Elements by ID

document.getElementById(id):
This method selects an element with a specific id attribute.

- Returns the first element with the matching id.
- Returns null if no element is found.

Example:
```
const heading =
document.getElementById("main-heading");
console.log(heading.textContent); // Logs
the text of the element with id="main-
heading"
```

2. Selecting Elements with CSS Selectors

document.querySelector(selector):
This method selects the **first** element that matches a specified CSS selector.

- Works with any valid CSS selector (.class, #id, [attribute], etc.).
- Returns null if no element matches.

Example:
```
const paragraph =
document.querySelector(".description");
```

```
console.log(paragraph.textContent); // Logs
the text of the first element with
class="description"
```

3. Selecting Multiple Elements

document.querySelectorAll(selector):

- Returns a NodeList containing all elements matching the CSS selector.
- Unlike getElementsByClassName, querySelectorAll does not live-update if the DOM changes.

Example:

```
const items =
document.querySelectorAll(".item");

items.forEach((item) =>
console.log(item.textContent)); // Logs the
text of all elements with class="item"
```

4. Differences Between getElementById and querySelector

- getElementById is faster but limited to selecting elements by id.
- querySelector is more flexible, supporting complex CSS selectors, but may be slightly slower.

5. Selecting Elements by Class Name

document.getElementsByClassName(className):

- Returns a live HTMLCollection of elements with the specified class name.
- If the DOM changes, the HTMLCollection updates automatically.

Example:

```
const buttons =
document.getElementsByClassName("btn");
```

```
console.log(buttons[0].textContent); //
Logs the text of the first button with
class="btn"
```

6. Selecting Elements by Tag Name

document.getElementsByTagName(tagName):

- Returns a live HTMLCollection of all elements with the specified tag name.

Example:

```
const divs =
document.getElementsByTagName("div");
```

```
console.log(divs.length); // Logs the
number of <div> elements in the document
```

7. Accessing Element Attributes

Once you select an element, you can access or modify its attributes.

- Use .getAttribute(attribute) to retrieve an attribute value.
- Use .setAttribute(attribute, value) to set an attribute value.

Example:

```
const link = document.querySelector("a");
```

```
console.log(link.getAttribute("href")); //
Logs the href attribute of the first <a>
element
```

```
link.setAttribute("target", "_blank"); //
Adds or modifies the target attribute
```

8. Accessing Element Text and HTML

- .textContent: Retrieves or sets the text inside an element.
- .innerHTML: Retrieves or sets the HTML inside an element.

Example:

```
const heading =
document.querySelector("h1");
console.log(heading.textContent); // Logs
plain text
heading.innerHTML = "<span>Updated
Text</span>"; // Sets HTML content
```

Multiple-Choice Questions

Which method would you use to select an element with a specific id?

1. `document.getElementById("id")`
2. `document.querySelector("#id")`
3. Both 1 and 2
4. `document.getElementByClass("id")`

Answer: 3. Both 1 and 2
Explanation: Both `getElementById` and `querySelector` can select elements by `id`, though `querySelector` requires a # prefix.

What does this code output if no element matches the selector?

```
const element =
document.querySelector(".nonexistent");
console.log(element);
```

1. `undefined`
2. `null`
3. `Error`
4. `" "`

Answer: 2. `null`
Explanation: If no element matches the selector, `querySelector` returns `null`.

What is the result of this code?

```
const element =
document.getElementById("header");
console.log(element.tagName);
```

1. "HEADER"
2. "header"
3. undefined
4. null

Answer: 1. "HEADER"
Explanation: The `tagName` property returns the uppercase tag name of the selected element.

What will this code output if there are two elements with the class btn?

```
const element =
document.querySelector(".btn");
console.log(element.textContent);
```

1. The text content of the first `.btn` element
2. The text content of the second `.btn` element
3. null
4. An array of the text contents of both elements

Answer: 1. The text content of the first `.btn` element
Explanation: `querySelector` selects the **first** matching element.

Which method returns all elements matching a CSS selector?

1. `document.querySelector`
2. `document.querySelectorAll`
3. `document.getElementsByClassName`
4. `document.getElementsByTagName`

Answer: 2. `document.querySelectorAll`
Explanation: The `querySelectorAll` method selects all elements matching a given CSS selector.

What does this code do?
```
const elements =
document.querySelectorAll("p");
console.log(elements.length);
```
1. Logs the number of <p> elements in the document
2. Logs the text content of the <p> elements
3. Throws an error
4. Returns `undefined`

Answer: 1. Logs the number of <p> elements in the document
Explanation: The `length` property of the `NodeList` returned by `querySelectorAll` indicates how many elements match the selector.

Which method should you use to access all <div> elements on a page?
1. `document.getElementById`
2. `document.getElementsByClassName`
3. `document.getElementsByTagName`
4. `document.querySelector`

Answer: 3. `document.getElementsByTagName`
Explanation: The `getElementsByTagName` method selects all elements with a specific tag name.

What is the main difference between getElementsByClassName and querySelectorAll?
1. `getElementsByClassName` supports CSS selectors.
2. `querySelectorAll` returns a live collection.

3. `getElementsByClassName` returns a live collection.
4. `querySelectorAll` only selects elements by class.

Answer: 3. `getElementsByClassName` returns a live collection.

Explanation: Unlike `querySelectorAll`, which returns a static `NodeList`, `getElementsByClassName` returns a live `HTMLCollection` that updates if the DOM changes.

What does this code output?

```
const element =
document.querySelector("#main");
console.log(element.textContent);
```

1. The text content of the element with `id="main"`
2. The HTML content of the element with `id="main"`
3. `undefined`
4. `null`

Answer: 1. The text content of the element with `id="main"`

Explanation: The `textContent` property retrieves the plain text inside the selected element.

What does this code do?

```
const link = document.querySelector("a");
link.setAttribute("href",
"https://example.com");
```

1. Changes the `href` attribute of the first `<a>` element
2. Retrieves the `href` attribute of the first `<a>` element
3. Logs the `href` attribute to the console
4. Throws an error

Answer: 1. Changes the `href` attribute of the first `<a>` element

Explanation: The `setAttribute` method modifies the value of an attribute on the selected element.

What does this code output?

```
const items =
document.querySelectorAll(".item");
console.log(items[1].textContent);
```

1. The text content of the first `.item` element
2. The text content of the second `.item` element
3. `undefined`
4. `Error`

Answer: 2. The text content of the second `.item` element
Explanation: The `querySelectorAll` method returns a `NodeList`, and you can access elements using array-like indexing.

Which method will always return an HTMLCollection?

1. `querySelectorAll`
2. `getElementsByClassName`
3. `getElementById`
4. `querySelector`

Answer: 2. `getElementsByClassName`
Explanation: The `getElementsByClassName` method returns a live `HTMLCollection`.

What will this code do?

```
const element =
document.querySelector("#main");
element.innerHTML = "<h2>New Content</h2>";
```

1. Updates the text content of the #main element
2. Replaces the content of the #main element with new HTML
3. Logs the current content of the #main element

4. Throws an error

Answer: 2. Replaces the content of the #main element with new HTML
Explanation: The innerHTML property sets the HTML content of the selected element.

What does this code output?

```
const elements =
document.getElementsByClassName("btn");
console.log(elements.length);
```

1. The number of elements with the class btn
2. The text content of all elements with the class btn
3. null
4. undefined

Answer: 1. The number of elements with the class btn
Explanation: The length property of the HTMLCollection indicates the number of matching elements.

What does document.querySelectorAll("div") return?

1. A single <div> element
2. All <div> elements as an HTMLCollection
3. All <div> elements as a NodeList
4. undefined

Answer: 3. All <div> elements as a NodeList
Explanation: The querySelectorAll method returns a static NodeList of all matching elements.

What happens if document.getElementById is called with an id that doesn't exist?

1. It throws an error.
2. It returns undefined.
3. It returns null.

4. It returns an empty object.

Answer: 3. It returns `null`.

Explanation: If no element matches the `id`, `getElementById` returns `null`.

What does this code do?

```
const button =
document.querySelector(".btn");
button.setAttribute("disabled", "");
```

1. Disables the button with the class `btn`
2. Removes the button with the class `btn`
3. Logs the current attributes of the button
4. Throws an error

Answer: 1. Disables the button with the class `btn`

Explanation: The `setAttribute` method adds or modifies an attribute on the selected element.

Which method returns only the first element that matches the CSS selector?

1. `getElementsByClassName`
2. `getElementsByTagName`
3. `querySelector`
4. `querySelectorAll`

Answer: 3. `querySelector`

Explanation: The `querySelector` method selects the first matching element.

What does this code output if the div exists?

```
const div = document.querySelector("div");
console.log(div.textContent);
```

1. The plain text content of the first `<div>`
2. The HTML content of the first `<div>`
3. The attributes of the first `<div>`

4. null

Answer: 1. The plain text content of the first `<div>`
Explanation: The `textContent` property retrieves only the text inside the element.

What does this code do?

```
const elements =
document.getElementsByTagName("li");
console.log(elements[0]);
```

1. Logs the first `<li>` element
2. Logs the text content of the first `<li>` element
3. Logs the total number of `<li>` elements
4. Throws an error

Answer: 1. Logs the first `<li>` element
Explanation: The `getElementsByTagName` method returns an `HTMLCollection`, and elements can be accessed using array-like indexing.

What will this code output?

```
const element =
document.querySelector("#main");
console.log(element.id);
```

1. The `id` of the selected element
2. The `id` of all elements in the document
3. `null`
4. `undefined`

Answer: 1. The `id` of the selected element
Explanation: The `id` property of an element returns its `id` attribute.

What does this code output?

```
const elements =
document.querySelectorAll(".item");
```

```
console.log(Array.isArray(elements));
```
1. true
2. false
3. undefined
4. Throws an error

Answer: 2. false

Explanation: The querySelectorAll method returns a NodeList, which is not an array.

What does this code do?
```
const element =
document.querySelector("#title");
element.textContent = "New Title";
```
1. Updates the HTML content of the #title element
2. Updates the text content of the #title element
3. Logs the current content of the #title element
4. Throws an error

Answer: 2. Updates the text content of the #title element

Explanation: The textContent property modifies the plain text inside the selected element.

What happens when you modify the innerHTML of an element?
1. It updates the plain text inside the element.
2. It updates the HTML content inside the element.
3. It removes all child elements.
4. It throws an error.

Answer: 2. It updates the HTML content inside the element.

Explanation: The innerHTML property sets the HTML content of the selected element.

What does this code output if the element exists?

```
const element =
document.getElementById("main");
console.log(element.className);
```

1. The class name(s) of the selected element
2. The id of the selected element
3. undefined
4. null

Answer: 1. The class name(s) of the selected element
Explanation: The className property retrieves or sets the class attribute of the element.

Modifying Element Content and Attributes in JavaScript

JavaScript allows you to dynamically modify the content and attributes of HTML elements, enabling interactive and dynamic web pages. This is done through the DOM (Document Object Model).

1. Modifying Content

1.1. textContent

- Updates or retrieves the text content of an element.
- Escapes HTML tags (treats them as plain text).

Example:

```
const heading =
document.querySelector("h1");
heading.textContent = "New Heading";
console.log(heading.textContent); //
Outputs: "New Heading"
```

1.2. innerHTML

- Updates or retrieves the HTML content of an element.

- Renders HTML tags as elements.

Example:

```
const div = document.querySelector("div");
div.innerHTML = "<strong>Bold
Text</strong>";
console.log(div.innerHTML); // Outputs:
"<strong>Bold Text</strong>"
```

1.3. innerText

- Similar to `textContent`, but it considers the rendered styles (e.g., hidden elements).

2. Modifying Attributes

2.1. setAttribute(attribute, value)

- Sets a specific attribute and its value.

Example:

```
const link = document.querySelector("a");
link.setAttribute("href",
"https://example.com");
```

2.2. getAttribute(attribute)

- Retrieves the value of a specific attribute.

Example:

```
console.log(link.getAttribute("href")); //
Outputs: "https://example.com"
```

2.3. removeAttribute(attribute)

- Removes a specified attribute.

Example:

```
link.removeAttribute("target");
```

2.4. Modifying Specific Attributes

- Attributes like `id`, `className`, `src`, and `alt` can be directly modified as properties.

Example:

```
const img = document.querySelector("img");
```

```
img.src = "new-image.jpg";
img.alt = "A new image";
```

3. Adding or Removing Classes

3.1. classList.add(className)

- Adds a class to the element.

Example:

```
const button =
document.querySelector("button");

button.classList.add("active");
```

3.2. classList.remove(className)

- Removes a class from the element.

Example:

```
button.classList.remove("inactive");
```

3.3. classList.toggle(className)

- Toggles a class on the element (adds it if absent, removes it if present).

Example:

```
button.classList.toggle("highlight");
```

4. Modifying Styles

4.1. Using the style Property

- Modifies inline styles of an element.

Example:

```
const box = document.querySelector(".box");

box.style.backgroundColor = "blue";

box.style.border = "2px solid black";
```

4.2. Using CSS Classes for Styles

- Modify or add CSS classes for better maintainability.

Multiple-Choice Questions

What does the textContent property do?

1. Retrieves or sets the text content of an element, including hidden elements.
2. Retrieves or sets the HTML content of an element.
3. Retrieves or sets the text content of an element, excluding hidden elements.
4. Removes the text content of an element.

Answer: 1. Retrieves or sets the text content of an element, including hidden elements.

Explanation: The textContent property works on all text within an element, regardless of visibility.

What does the innerHTML property do?

1. Retrieves or sets the plain text content of an element.
2. Escapes HTML tags as plain text.
3. Retrieves or sets the HTML content of an element.
4. Removes all children of the element.

Answer: 3. Retrieves or sets the HTML content of an element.

Explanation: The innerHTML property renders HTML tags as elements and sets or retrieves the content.

What happens when innerHTML is set to a string containing HTML?

1. Updates the plain text inside the element.
2. Updates the HTML inside the element.
3. Throws an error.
4. Adds the HTML as a sibling element.

Answer: 2. Updates the HTML inside the element.

Explanation: Setting innerHTML replaces the current HTML content of the element with the new content.

What does this code do?

```
const link = document.querySelector("a");
link.setAttribute("target", "_blank");
```

1. Changes the href attribute of the link.
2. Sets the target attribute to open the link in a new tab.
3. Logs the target attribute of the link.
4. Throws an error.

Answer: 2. Sets the target attribute to open the link in a new tab.

Explanation: The setAttribute method modifies or adds the specified attribute.

What is the output of this code?

```
const div = document.querySelector("div");
div.textContent = "<strong>Hello</strong>";
console.log(div.textContent);
```

1. `<strong>Hello</strong>`
2. `Hello`
3. `undefined`
4. `null`

Answer: 1. `<strong>Hello</strong>`

Explanation: The textContent property treats the string as plain text, not HTML.

Which method removes an attribute from an element?

1. `removeAttribute`
2. `setAttribute`
3. `deleteAttribute`
4. `clearAttribute`

Answer: 1. `removeAttribute`
Explanation: The `removeAttribute` method deletes the specified attribute from the element.

What does this code do?

```
const img = document.querySelector("img");
img.src = "new-image.jpg";
```

1. Changes the `alt` attribute of the image.
2. Changes the `src` attribute to display a new image.
3. Removes the `src` attribute from the image.
4. Throws an error.

Answer: 2. Changes the `src` attribute to display a new image.
Explanation: The `src` property updates the source URL of the image.

What happens when you use classList.add("new-class")?

1. Replaces all existing classes with `new-class`.
2. Adds `new-class` to the element if it doesn't already exist.
3. Toggles the presence of `new-class`.
4. Removes `new-class` from the element.

Answer: 2. Adds `new-class` to the element if it doesn't already exist.
Explanation: The `classList.add` method adds the class only if it's not already present.

What does the following code output?

```
const link = document.querySelector("a");
console.log(link.getAttribute("href"));
```

1. The `href` attribute value of the link
2. The inner HTML of the link

3. `null`
4. Throws an error

Answer: 1. The `href` attribute value of the link
Explanation: The `getAttribute` method retrieves the value of the specified attribute.

What does this code do?

```
const box = document.querySelector(".box");
box.style.backgroundColor = "red";
```

1. Changes the text color to red.
2. Changes the background color of the .box element to red.
3. Throws an error.
4. Logs the current background color.

Answer: 2. Changes the background color of the .box element to red.
Explanation: The `style` property modifies the inline styles of the element.

What does the innerText property do?

1. Retrieves or sets the plain text of an element, including hidden elements.
2. Retrieves or sets the HTML content of an element.
3. Retrieves or sets the text content of an element, excluding hidden elements.
4. Removes the text content of an element.

Answer: 3. Retrieves or sets the text content of an element, excluding hidden elements.
Explanation: The `innerText` property retrieves or sets the visible text content of an element, ignoring hidden elements.

What is the purpose of the classList.toggle method?

1. Replaces the existing class with a new class.

2. Adds the class if it doesn't exist, otherwise removes it.
3. Removes all classes from the element.
4. Throws an error if the class doesn't exist.

Answer: 2. Adds the class if it doesn't exist, otherwise removes it.

Explanation: The `toggle` method alternates the presence of a class on an element.

What does this code output?

```
const div = document.querySelector("div");
div.innerHTML = "<p>Hello</p>";
console.log(div.textContent);
```

1. `<p>Hello</p>`
2. `Hello`
3. `undefined`
4. `null`

Answer: 2. `Hello`

Explanation: The `innerHTML` property sets the HTML content, and `textContent` retrieves the plain text inside the element.

Which method can remove all child elements from a DOM node?

1. `node.clear()`
2. `node.removeAll()`
3. `node.innerHTML = ""`
4. `node.deleteChildren()`

Answer: 3. `node.innerHTML = ""`

Explanation: Setting `innerHTML` to an empty string removes all child elements from the node.

What does this code do?

```
const button =
document.querySelector("button");
button.classList.remove("active");
```

1. Removes all classes from the button.
2. Removes the `active` class from the button if it exists.
3. Throws an error if the `active` class doesn't exist.
4. Adds the `active` class to the button.

Answer: 2. Removes the `active` class from the button if it exists.
Explanation: The `classList.remove` method only removes the specified class if it is present.

What will this code output?

```
const img = document.querySelector("img");
console.log(img.alt);
```

1. The `alt` attribute value of the image
2. The `src` attribute value of the image
3. `null`
4. `undefined`

Answer: 1. The `alt` attribute value of the image
Explanation: The `alt` property retrieves the value of the `alt` attribute.

What happens when removeAttribute("class") is used on an element?

1. Removes a specific class from the element.
2. Removes all classes from the element.
3. Removes the `class` attribute entirely from the element.
4. Throws an error if no classes exist.

Answer: 3. Removes the `class` attribute entirely from the element.
Explanation: The `removeAttribute` method deletes the entire `class` attribute, removing all classes.

Which property allows you to modify an element's inline styles directly?

1. `classList`
2. `style`
3. `attributes`
4. `innerHTML`

Answer: 2. `style`
Explanation: The `style` property is used to directly modify inline CSS properties.

What is the output of this code?

```
const link = document.querySelector("a");
link.setAttribute("href",
"https://example.com");
console.log(link.href);
```

1. `https://example.com`
2. The relative path to the link
3. `undefined`
4. `null`

Answer: 1. `https://example.com`
Explanation: The `href` property reflects the fully resolved URL of the link.

What will this code do?

```
const element =
document.querySelector(".box");
element.style.display = "none";
```

1. Hides the `.box` element.

2. Removes the `.box` element from the DOM.
3. Throws an error.
4. Changes the color of the `.box` element.

Answer: 1. Hides the `.box` element.
Explanation: Setting `display` to `"none"` makes the element invisible but keeps it in the DOM.

What does the setAttribute method do?
1. Removes an attribute from an element.
2. Adds or updates an attribute on an element.
3. Retrieves the value of an attribute.
4. Checks if an attribute exists.

Answer: 2. Adds or updates an attribute on an element.
Explanation: The `setAttribute` method assigns a value to the specified attribute, creating it if it doesn't exist.

What happens if you set innerHTML with user-provided content?
1. The content is sanitized automatically.
2. Only plain text is added.
3. It might expose the site to cross-site scripting (XSS) attacks.
4. It throws an error.

Answer: 3. It might expose the site to cross-site scripting (XSS) attacks.
Explanation: Setting `innerHTML` with untrusted content can introduce security vulnerabilities.

What does this code do?

```
const element =
document.querySelector("#title");
element.id = "new-title";
```

1. Adds a new attribute to the element.
2. Modifies the element's `id` attribute to `"new-title"`.

3. Removes the `id` attribute from the element.
4. Throws an error.

Answer: 2. Modifies the element's `id` attribute to `"new-title"`.

Explanation: The `id` property directly modifies the `id` attribute of the element.

What does this code do?
```
const box = document.querySelector(".box");
box.style.border = "1px solid black";
```
1. Adds a border to the `.box` element.
2. Logs the current border style of the `.box` element.
3. Removes the border from the `.box` element.
4. Throws an error.

Answer: 1. Adds a border to the `.box` element.

Explanation: The `style` property allows you to add or modify inline styles, including borders.

What will this code output?
```
const div = document.querySelector("div");
div.innerHTML = "<h1>Hello</h1>";
console.log(div.innerHTML);
```
1. `<h1>Hello</h1>`
2. `Hello`
3. `undefined`
4. `null`

Answer: 1. `<h1>Hello</h1>`

Explanation: The `innerHTML` property retrieves the HTML content of the element, including tags.

Adding and Removing DOM Elements Dynamically in JavaScript

Dynamically modifying the DOM is a core capability of JavaScript, allowing you to add, remove, or rearrange elements on a webpage without requiring a reload. This is essential for creating interactive and responsive web applications.

1. Adding Elements to the DOM

1.1. Creating New Elements

- Use document.createElement(tagName) to create a new DOM element.

Example:

```
const newDiv =
document.createElement("div");
```

1.2. Adding Elements to the DOM

- Use methods like appendChild or append to add elements to a parent node.

Example:

```
const parent =
document.querySelector("#container");

const newDiv =
document.createElement("div");

newDiv.textContent = "Hello, World!";

parent.appendChild(newDiv); // Adds newDiv
as the last child of #container
```

- **appendChild(newNode)**: Adds a single node as a child of the parent node.
- **append(...nodes)**: Adds one or more nodes or strings as children.

1.3. Inserting Elements at Specific Positions

- Use `insertBefore(newNode, referenceNode)` to insert an element before a specific child.

Example:

```
const reference =
document.querySelector("#item2");

const newItem =
document.createElement("li");

newItem.textContent = "New Item";

reference.parentNode.insertBefore(newItem,
reference);
```

1.4. Adding HTML with `innerHTML`

- Set `innerHTML` on an element to insert raw HTML. **Example**:

```
document.body.innerHTML += "<p>Added
Paragraph</p>";
```

2. Removing Elements from the DOM

2.1. Removing Child Nodes

- Use `parentNode.removeChild(childNode)` to remove a child element.

Example:

```
const item =
document.querySelector("#itemToRemove");

item.parentNode.removeChild(item);
```

2.2. Removing Elements Directly

- Use `element.remove()` to remove an element directly.

Example:

```
const item =
document.querySelector("#itemToRemove");

item.remove();
```

2.3. Clearing All Child Nodes

- To remove all child elements, you can loop through them or set innerHTML to an empty string.

Example:

```
const container =
document.querySelector("#container");

container.innerHTML = ""; // Clears all
child elements
```

3. Replacing Elements

3.1. Replace a Child Node

- Use parentNode.replaceChild(newNode, oldNode).

Example:

```
const oldItem =
document.querySelector("#oldItem");

const newItem =
document.createElement("p");

newItem.textContent = "New Content";

oldItem.parentNode.replaceChild(newItem,
oldItem);
```

Multiple-Choice Questions

What does the document.createElement method do?

1. Creates a new element and adds it to the DOM.
2. Creates a new element but does not add it to the DOM.
3. Deletes an element from the DOM.
4. Finds an element by its tag name.

Answer: 2. Creates a new element but does not add it to the DOM.

Explanation: The createElement method creates a new DOM element but doesn't attach it to the document until explicitly added.

Which method adds a new child element to the end of a parent node?

1. `appendChild`
2. `insertBefore`
3. `replaceChild`
4. `removeChild`

Answer: 1. `appendChild`
Explanation: The `appendChild` method adds a new child node to the end of the parent node's children.

What does this code do?

```
const parent =
document.querySelector("#container");
const newDiv =
document.createElement("div");
newDiv.textContent = "Hello";
parent.appendChild(newDiv);
```

1. Creates and appends a new `<div>` with text content `"Hello"` to the parent with `id="container"`.
2. Creates and inserts a new `<div>` before the first child of `#container`.
3. Throws an error because `appendChild` is not valid for `div` elements.
4. Replaces the content of `#container` with the new `<div>`.

Answer: 1. Creates and appends a new `<div>` with text content `"Hello"` to the parent with `id="container"`.
Explanation: The `appendChild` method appends the new `<div>` to the `#container` element.

Which method inserts a new element before an existing one?

1. `appendChild`
2. `insertBefore`
3. `replaceChild`
4. `removeChild`

Answer: 2. `insertBefore`
Explanation: The `insertBefore` method inserts a node before a specified reference node.

What does this code do?

```
const item =
document.querySelector("#item");
item.remove();
```

1. Removes the element with `id="item"` from the DOM.
2. Removes all children of the element with `id="item"`.
3. Throws an error because `remove()` is not a valid method.
4. Clears the content of the element with `id="item"`.

Answer: 1. Removes the element with `id="item"` from the DOM.
Explanation: The `remove()` method removes the selected element directly from the DOM.

What is the purpose of replaceChild?

1. Adds a new child element to a parent.
2. Removes a child element from a parent.
3. Replaces an existing child element with a new one.
4. Clears all child elements from a parent.

Answer: 3. Replaces an existing child element with a new one.

Explanation: The `replaceChild` method swaps an existing child with a new element.

What does this code output?

```
const list = document.querySelector("ul");
list.innerHTML += "<li>New Item</li>";
```

1. Appends a new `<li>` element with text "New Item" to the list.
2. Replaces all child elements of the list with a new `<li>` element.
3. Throws an error because `innerHTML` cannot be used with `<ul>`.
4. Removes all `<li>` elements from the list.

Answer: 1. Appends a new `<li>` element with text "New Item" to the list.
Explanation: Using += with `innerHTML` appends new content while preserving existing content.

What does this code do?

```
const parent =
document.querySelector("#container");
while (parent.firstChild) {
  parent.removeChild(parent.firstChild);
}
```

1. Removes all child elements from `#container`.
2. Throws an error because `removeChild` cannot be used in a loop.
3. Removes only the first child of `#container`.
4. Appends all children of `#container` to the document body.

Answer: 1. Removes all child elements from `#container`.
Explanation: The `while` loop iterates until all child elements are removed from the parent node.

Which method can directly remove a DOM element?

1. `removeChild`
2. `remove`
3. Both 1 and 2
4. `replaceChild`

Answer: 3. Both 1 and 2

Explanation: Both `removeChild` (when called on the parent) and `remove` (when called on the element) can remove a DOM element.

What happens if you call innerHTML = "" on an element?

1. It removes all child elements from the element.
2. It throws an error.
3. It appends a blank `<div>` to the element.
4. It hides the element but keeps its content.

Answer: 1. It removes all child elements from the element.

Explanation: Setting `innerHTML` to an empty string clears all content inside the element.

What will this code output?

```
const parent =
document.querySelector("#list");
const item = document.createElement("li");
item.textContent = "Item 4";
parent.appendChild(item);
console.log(parent.children.length);
```

1. Adds "Item 4" to the list and logs the updated number of children.
2. Throws an error because `appendChild` cannot be used with `<li>`.
3. Replaces the last child of the list with "Item 4".
4. Removes all children from the parent node.

Answer: 1. Adds "Item 4" to the list and logs the updated number of children.
Explanation: The appendChild method adds the new `<li>` as a child, increasing the number of children.

What does parentNode.removeChild(childNode) do?

1. Removes a specified child node from the parent node.
2. Removes the parent node entirely from the DOM.
3. Clears all attributes of the child node.
4. Throws an error if the child node doesn't exist.

Answer: 1. Removes a specified child node from the parent node.
Explanation: The removeChild method removes the specified child node.

What happens if the reference node in insertBefore(newNode, referenceNode) is null?

1. Throws an error.
2. Inserts the new node as the first child.
3. Inserts the new node as the last child.
4. Removes the reference node.

Answer: 3. Inserts the new node as the last child.
Explanation: If the referenceNode is null, insertBefore places the new node at the end of the parent's child list.

What does this code do?

```
const parent =
document.querySelector("#container");
const newDiv =
document.createElement("div");
newDiv.textContent = "New Element";
parent.insertBefore(newDiv,
parent.firstChild);
```

1. Adds the new <div> as the last child of #container.
2. Adds the new <div> as the first child of #container.
3. Throws an error if firstChild is null.
4. Replaces the first child of #container.

Answer: 2. Adds the new <div> as the first child of #container.
Explanation: The insertBefore method places the new <div> before the firstChild.

What does element.remove() do?
1. Removes the specified element from the DOM.
2. Removes all children of the specified element.
3. Clears all attributes of the specified element.
4. Logs the content of the element.

Answer: 1. Removes the specified element from the DOM.
Explanation: The remove() method directly removes the element on which it is called.

What is the result of this code?
```
const ul = document.querySelector("ul");
ul.innerHTML = "<li>New Item</li>";
```
1. Replaces all <li> elements in the list with a single <li> element.
2. Appends a new <li> to the existing list.
3. Throws an error if the <ul> already has children.
4. Clears all child elements of the list.

Answer: 1. Replaces all <li> elements in the list with a single <li> element.
Explanation: Setting innerHTML replaces the current content of the element.

What does this code output?

```
const parent =
document.querySelector("#container");
console.log(parent.firstChild);
```

1. Logs the first child node of the parent element.
2. Logs the first child element of the parent element.
3. Logs the last child node of the parent element.
4. Logs `null`.

Answer: 1. Logs the first child node of the parent element.
Explanation: The `firstChild` property retrieves the first child node, which can include text nodes.

What happens if you set innerHTML = "" on an element?

1. The element is removed from the DOM.
2. The content of the element is cleared.
3. All attributes of the element are removed.
4. Throws an error.

Answer: 2. The content of the element is cleared.
Explanation: Setting `innerHTML` to an empty string clears the content but leaves the element in the DOM.

Which of the following is the most efficient way to remove all children of a DOM node?

1. `node.remove()`
2. `node.innerHTML = ""`
3. `node.parentNode.removeChild(node)`
4. `while (node.firstChild) {`
   `node.removeChild(node.firstChild); }`

Answer: 2. `node.innerHTML = ""`
Explanation: Setting `innerHTML` to an empty string clears all child nodes in a single operation.

What will this code do?

```
const list = document.querySelector("ul");
const newItem =
document.createElement("li");
newItem.textContent = "Item 4";
list.appendChild(newItem);
```

1. Adds a new <li> element as the last child of the <ul>.
2. Replaces the last child of the <ul> with the new <li>.
3. Adds the new <li> element before the first child of the <ul>.
4. Throws an error.

Answer: 1. Adds a new <li> element as the last child of the <ul>.

Explanation: The appendChild method adds the new <li> to the end of the list.

Which method should you use to replace a child element?

1. appendChild
2. insertBefore
3. replaceChild
4. removeChild

Answer: 3. replaceChild

Explanation: The replaceChild method replaces an existing child with a new one.

What does this code output?

```
const parent =
document.querySelector("#list");
console.log(parent.childNodes.length);
```

1. The number of all child nodes, including text and comment nodes.
2. The number of child elements only.
3. The number of child text nodes only.
4. Throws an error.

Answer: 1. The number of all child nodes, including text and comment nodes.
Explanation: The childNodes property includes all types of nodes, not just elements.

What happens if document.createElement("div") is not appended to the DOM?
1. It exists in memory but is not visible on the webpage.
2. It is automatically appended to the <body>.
3. It throws an error.
4. It replaces the first <div> on the page.

Answer: 1. It exists in memory but is not visible on the webpage.
Explanation: The element is created in memory and must be explicitly added to the DOM to appear on the page.

Which of the following methods is used to check if an element has child nodes?
1. hasChildNodes()
2. childNodes.length
3. children.length
4. firstChild

Answer: 1. hasChildNodes()
Explanation: The hasChildNodes() method returns true if the element has any child nodes, including text and comments.

What does this code do?

```
const oldItem =
document.querySelector("#item");
const newItem =
document.createElement("li");
newItem.textContent = "New Item";
oldItem.parentNode.replaceChild(newItem,
oldItem);
```

1. Replaces #item with the new \<li> element.
2. Appends the new \<li> element as the last child of #item.
3. Removes the #item element without adding anything.
4. Throws an error.

Answer: 1. Replaces #item with the new \<li> element.
Explanation: The replaceChild method swaps the old child with the new one.

Adding and Removing Event Listeners in JavaScript

Event listeners allow JavaScript to respond to user interactions, system events, or other changes on a webpage. They enable developers to make web pages interactive by executing specific code when an event occurs, such as a click, hover, or key press.

1. Adding Event Listeners

1.1. addEventListener Method

The addEventListener method is used to attach an event handler to a DOM element.

Syntax:

```
element.addEventListener(eventType,
eventHandler, useCapture);
```

Example:

```
const button =
document.querySelector("button");
button.addEventListener("click", () => {
  console.log("Button clicked!");
});
```

- **eventType**: A string representing the event type (e.g., `"click"`, `"mouseover"`, `"keydown"`).
- **eventHandler**: A function to execute when the event occurs.
- **useCapture (optional)**: A Boolean indicating whether the event should be captured during the capturing or bubbling phase (default is `false`).

2. Removing Event Listeners

2.1. removeEventListener Method

The `removeEventListener` method detaches an event handler from an element.

Syntax:

```
element.removeEventListener(eventType,
eventHandler, useCapture);
```

Example:

```
const button =
document.querySelector("button");
function handleClick() {
  console.log("Button clicked!");
}
button.addEventListener("click",
handleClick);
button.removeEventListener("click",
handleClick);
```

191

3. Key Points to Remember

Named Functions: To remove an event listener, you must pass the exact same function reference used when adding it. Anonymous functions cannot be removed.

```
button.addEventListener("click",
handleClick); // Can be removed
```

```
button.addEventListener("click", () =>
console.log("Clicked!")); // Cannot be
removed
```

Event Object: Most event handlers receive an event object containing details about the event.

```
button.addEventListener("click", (event) =>
{
  console.log(event.type); // Logs "click"
});
```

1. **Event Phases**: Events have two main phases:
   o **Capturing Phase**: The event travels from the root to the target.
   o **Bubbling Phase**: The event bubbles up from the target to the root.
   o Use useCapture to specify the phase in which the listener should execute.

Multiple-Choice Questions

What is the purpose of the addEventListener method?

1. To execute a function immediately.
2. To attach an event handler to a DOM element.
3. To remove an event handler from a DOM element.
4. To trigger an event manually.

Answer: 2. To attach an event handler to a DOM element.
Explanation: The addEventListener method attaches an event handler to an element that executes when the specified event occurs.

192

Which of the following is the correct syntax for adding an event listener?

1. `element.addEventListener("click", myFunction);`
2. `element.attachEvent("click", myFunction);`
3. `element.addEventHandler("click", myFunction);`
4. `element.on("click", myFunction);`

Answer: 1. `element.addEventListener("click", myFunction);`
Explanation: The correct method to add an event listener is `addEventListener`, which takes the event type and handler as arguments.

What happens if you pass an anonymous function to addEventListener and try to remove it later?

1. It throws an error.
2. The anonymous function is successfully removed.
3. The anonymous function cannot be removed.
4. The event listener is disabled temporarily.

Answer: 3. The anonymous function cannot be removed.
Explanation: You cannot remove an anonymous function because `removeEventListener` requires the same function reference that was passed to `addEventListener`.

What does this code do?

```
const button =
document.querySelector("button");
button.addEventListener("mouseover", () =>
{
  console.log("Mouse is over the button!");
});
```

1. Executes the handler when the button is clicked.
2. Executes the handler when the mouse moves over the button.
3. Executes the handler when the button loses focus.
4. Throws an error.

Answer: 2. Executes the handler when the mouse moves over the button.

Explanation: The `"mouseover"` event triggers when the mouse enters the element.

What is the third parameter in addEventListener used for?

1. To specify the type of event.
2. To pass arguments to the event handler.
3. To indicate whether the event should be captured or bubbled.
4. To disable the event listener.

Answer: 3. To indicate whether the event should be captured or bubbled.

Explanation: The third parameter determines whether the event handler should execute during the capturing phase (`true`) or the bubbling phase (`false`).

What does this code output when the button is clicked?

```
const button =
document.querySelector("button");
button.addEventListener("click", (event) =>
{
  console.log(event.type);
});
```

1. `click`
2. The ID of the button
3. `undefined`
4. Throws an error

Answer: 1. `click`
Explanation: The `type` property of the event object contains the event type.

How do you remove an event listener?

1. `element.detachEvent(eventType, eventHandler);`
2. `element.off(eventType, eventHandler);`
3. `element.removeEventListener(eventType, eventHandler);`
4. `element.removeHandler(eventType, eventHandler);`

Answer: 3.
`element.removeEventListener(eventType, eventHandler);`
Explanation: The `removeEventListener` method removes an event listener attached to the element.

What does this code do?

```
const handleClick = () =>
console.log("Clicked!");
button.addEventListener("click",
handleClick);
button.removeEventListener("click",
handleClick);
```

1. Attaches and immediately removes the click event listener.
2. Attaches the event listener permanently.
3. Throws an error because `removeEventListener` is invalid.
4. Prevents the button from being clicked.

Answer: 1. Attaches and immediately removes the click event listener.
Explanation: The event listener is added and then removed, so the handler does not execute.

195

What happens if the same event listener is added twice to an element?

1. It throws an error.
2. The event listener executes only once.
3. The event listener executes twice.
4. The second addition overrides the first.

Answer: 3. The event listener executes twice.
Explanation: Adding the same listener twice results in the handler being called twice.

What does this code output?

```
const button =
document.querySelector("button");
button.addEventListener("click", () => {
  console.log("Clicked!");
});
button.addEventListener("click", () => {
  console.log("Clicked again!");
});
```

1. Logs "Clicked!" only once.
2. Logs "Clicked!" followed by "Clicked again!".
3. Logs "Clicked again!" only.
4. Throws an error.

Answer: 2. Logs "Clicked!" followed by "Clicked again!".
Explanation: Multiple listeners can be attached to the same event, and they execute in the order they are added.

Which of the following event types would you use to listen for a key press?

1. "keypress"
2. "keydown"

3. `"keyup"`
4. All of the above

Answer: 4. All of the above
Explanation: `"keypress"`, `"keydown"`, and `"keyup"` are all valid keyboard events, each triggering at different stages of a key interaction.

What happens when useCapture is set to true in addEventListener?

1. The event is handled during the bubbling phase.
2. The event is handled during the capturing phase.
3. The event handler is disabled.
4. The event listener is added twice.

Answer: 2. The event is handled during the capturing phase.
Explanation: When `useCapture` is `true`, the listener handles the event during the capturing phase.

Which of the following statements is true about removeEventListener?

1. It works even if the `useCapture` parameter is different from the one used in `addEventListener`.
2. It only works if the exact same function reference and parameters are used.
3. It works for both named and anonymous functions.
4. It removes all event listeners from the element.

Answer: 2. It only works if the exact same function reference and parameters are used.
Explanation: To remove an event listener, `removeEventListener` requires the same function reference and `useCapture` parameter as were used when adding it.

What is the role of the event.preventDefault() method inside an event handler?

1. Stops the event from bubbling up.
2. Cancels the default behavior of the event.
3. Removes the event listener.
4. Logs the event to the console.

Answer: 2. Cancels the default behavior of the event.
Explanation: The `preventDefault` method stops the browser's default action for the event (e.g., following a link).

What does this code output?

```
const button =
document.querySelector("button");
button.addEventListener("click", (event) =>
{
  event.preventDefault();
  console.log("Default prevented!");
});
```

1. `"Default prevented!"`
2. Logs nothing but prevents the default action.
3. Throws an error.
4. Logs the event object.

Answer: 1. `"Default prevented!"`
Explanation: The event handler prevents the default action and logs the specified message.

What does stopPropagation() do?

1. Prevents the event from triggering other handlers on the same element.
2. Prevents the event from moving to the next phase (bubbling or capturing).
3. Removes the event listener.
4. Cancels the default behavior of the event.

Answer: 2. Prevents the event from moving to the next phase (bubbling or capturing).
Explanation: The stopPropagation method stops the event from propagating to other listeners.

What happens if two event listeners are added to the same element for the same event, one in the capturing phase and one in the bubbling phase?
1. Only the capturing listener executes.
2. Only the bubbling listener executes.
3. Both listeners execute, starting with the capturing listener.
4. Both listeners execute, starting with the bubbling listener.

Answer: 3. Both listeners execute, starting with the capturing listener.
Explanation: Capturing listeners execute before bubbling listeners.

What does this code do?
```
const div = document.querySelector("div");
div.addEventListener("click", (event) => {
  console.log("Div clicked!");
  event.stopPropagation();
});
document.body.addEventListener("click", ()
=> {
  console.log("Body clicked!");
});
```
1. Logs "Div clicked!" and "Body clicked!" when the div is clicked.
2. Logs only "Div clicked!" when the div is clicked.
3. Throws an error because stopPropagation is invalid.

4. Logs "`Body clicked!`" when the div is clicked.

Answer: 2. Logs only "`Div clicked!`" when the div is clicked.

Explanation: The `stopPropagation` method prevents the event from propagating to the body.

What does this code do?
```
const link = document.querySelector("a");
link.addEventListener("click", (event) => {
  event.preventDefault();
  console.log("Link clicked but not
followed!");
});
```
  1. Prevents the link from navigating to its `href`.
  2. Executes the default behavior of the link.
  3. Throws an error.
  4. Logs nothing and follows the link.

Answer: 1. Prevents the link from navigating to its `href`.

Explanation: The `preventDefault` method cancels the default navigation behavior.

What happens if you call removeEventListener with a useCapture value different from addEventListener?
  1. The event listener is still removed.
  2. The event listener is not removed.
  3. It throws an error.
  4. It removes all event listeners for the event type.

Answer: 2. The event listener is not removed.

Explanation: The `useCapture` parameter must match exactly between `addEventListener` and `removeEventListener`.

What does this code output when clicking the button?

```
const button =
document.querySelector("button");
function handleClick(event) {
  console.log(event.target);
}
button.addEventListener("click",
handleClick);
button.removeEventListener("click",
handleClick);
button.click();
```

1. Logs the button element.
2. Logs `null`.
3. Throws an error.
4. Logs nothing.

Answer: 4. Logs nothing.
Explanation: The `removeEventListener` method removes the event handler, so it doesn't execute when the button is clicked.

Which of the following is true about event delegation?

1. It requires adding listeners to multiple elements.
2. It uses a parent element to handle events for child elements.
3. It only works for `click` events.
4. It is slower than adding individual event listeners.

Answer: 2. It uses a parent element to handle events for child elements.
Explanation: Event delegation takes advantage of event bubbling by attaching a single listener to a parent element.

What does this code do?

```
document.addEventListener("click", (event)
=> {
```

```
if (event.target.matches(".btn")) {
    console.log("Button clicked!");
  }
});
```

1. Executes for any click event on the document.
2. Executes only for elements with the class .btn.
3. Throws an error because matches is not a valid method.
4. Logs nothing.

Answer: 2. Executes only for elements with the class .btn.

Explanation: The matches method checks if the clicked element matches the selector.

What is the purpose of the once option in addEventListener?

1. To add the listener only during the capturing phase.
2. To ensure the listener executes only once and then removes itself.
3. To prevent event propagation.
4. To delay the execution of the event handler.

Answer: 2. To ensure the listener executes only once and then removes itself.

Explanation: The once option ensures the handler runs a single time and is then automatically removed.

What does this code do?

```
const button =
document.querySelector("button");
button.addEventListener("click", () => {
    console.log("Clicked!");
}, { once: true });
button.click();
button.click();
```

1. Logs "Clicked!" twice.
2. Logs "Clicked!" once.
3. Logs nothing.
4. Throws an error.

Answer: 2. Logs "Clicked!" once.

Explanation: The once option ensures the handler runs only for the first click and is then removed.

Event Propagation and Delegation in JavaScript

JavaScript events follow a structured flow within the DOM, known as **event propagation**, which includes two main phases: **capturing** and **bubbling**. Event delegation leverages this flow to efficiently handle events on multiple child elements using a single event listener on a parent.

1. Event Propagation

1.1. Capturing Phase

- The event travels from the root of the DOM tree down to the target element.
- Also known as the "trickle-down phase."
- Event listeners in this phase execute if useCapture is set to true when adding the listener.

Example:

```
document.body.addEventListener(
  "click",
  () => console.log("Capturing phase"),
  true
);
```

1.2. Target Phase
- The event reaches the target element, where event listeners on the target execute.

1.3. Bubbling Phase
- The event bubbles back up the DOM tree, starting from the target to the root.
- Event listeners execute by default during this phase.

Example:

```
document.body.addEventListener("click", ()
=> console.log("Bubbling phase"));
```

2. Stopping Event Propagation

2.1. event.stopPropagation()
- Prevents the event from propagating further in either the capturing or bubbling phase.

Example:

```
document.querySelector("#child").addEventLi
stener("click", (event) => {
  event.stopPropagation();
  console.log("Child clicked, propagation
stopped!");
});
```

2.2. event.stopImmediatePropagation()
- Prevents the event from propagating and blocks other listeners on the same element.

3. Event Delegation
Event delegation leverages event propagation (bubbling phase) to handle events for multiple child elements by attaching a single event listener to their parent.

Example:

```
document.querySelector("#list").addEventLis
tener("click", (event) => {
  if (event.target.tagName === "LI") {
    console.log(`Item clicked:
${event.target.textContent}`);
  }
});
```

4. Key Differences: Capturing vs Bubbling

Phase	Execution	Default Behavior
Capturing Phase	Root → Target	Requires useCapture: true
Bubbling Phase	Target → Root	Default for most events

Multiple-Choice Questions

What is the correct order of phases in event propagation?
1. Capturing → Target → Bubbling
2. Bubbling → Target → Capturing
3. Target → Capturing → Bubbling
4. Capturing → Bubbling → Target

Answer: 1. Capturing → Target → Bubbling
Explanation: Event propagation starts with the capturing phase, reaches the target, and then proceeds with the bubbling phase.

What is the default phase for most event listeners?
1. Capturing
2. Bubbling

3. Target
4. None

Answer: 2. Bubbling
Explanation: By default, event listeners execute during the bubbling phase.

What does the event.stopPropagation() method do?
1. Stops the event from reaching the target element.
2. Prevents the event from propagating in the bubbling phase.
3. Stops all listeners from executing on the target element.
4. Cancels the default action of the event.

Answer: 2. Prevents the event from propagating in the bubbling phase.
Explanation: stopPropagation() prevents the event from continuing to propagate through the DOM hierarchy.

Which method prevents an event from propagating and blocks other listeners on the same element?
1. event.preventDefault()
2. event.stopPropagation()
3. event.stopImmediatePropagation()
4. event.cancel()

Answer: 3. event.stopImmediatePropagation()
Explanation: This method stops the event from propagating and prevents other event listeners on the same element from executing.

Which of the following best describes event delegation?
1. Attaching listeners to multiple elements individually.
2. Adding a single listener to a parent element to handle events for its child elements.
3. Using stopPropagation to delegate events.

4. Handling events during the capturing phase only.

Answer: 2. Adding a single listener to a parent element to handle events for its child elements.

Explanation: Event delegation relies on the bubbling phase to handle events for multiple child elements with a single parent listener.

What does this code do?

```
document.querySelector("#parent").addEventL
istener("click", (event) => {
  console.log(`Clicked:
${event.target.tagName}`);
});
```

1. Logs the tag name of the parent element.
2. Logs the tag name of the element that triggered the event.
3. Prevents the event from bubbling.
4. Throws an error.

Answer: 2. Logs the tag name of the element that triggered the event.

Explanation: The event.target property references the element that triggered the event.

Which property identifies the element where the event handler is attached?

1. `event.target`
2. `event.currentTarget`
3. `event.source`
4. `event.handler`

Answer: 2. `event.currentTarget`

Explanation: The currentTarget property refers to the element to which the event listener is attached.

What is the purpose of the useCapture parameter in addEventListener?

1. Specifies the order of event listeners.
2. Executes the listener during the capturing phase if `true`.
3. Executes the listener during the bubbling phase if `true`.
4. Stops the event propagation.

Answer: 2. Executes the listener during the capturing phase if `true`.

Explanation: The `useCapture` parameter determines if the listener executes during the capturing phase.

What does this code output when clicking the child element?

```
document.body.addEventListener("click", ()
=> console.log("Body clicked!"), true);
document.querySelector("#child").addEventLi
stener("click", () => console.log("Child
clicked!"));
```

1. `Body clicked!` → `Child clicked!`
2. `Child clicked!` → `Body clicked!`
3. Only `Body clicked!`
4. Only `Child clicked!`

Answer: 1. `Body clicked!` → `Child clicked!`

Explanation: The `useCapture: true` causes the body listener to execute during the capturing phase, before the child listener.

What is a key advantage of event delegation?

1. It prevents bubbling automatically.
2. It requires fewer event listeners, improving performance.
3. It works only during the capturing phase.

4. It cancels the default action of the event.

Answer: 2. It requires fewer event listeners, improving performance.
Explanation: Event delegation minimizes the number of event listeners by attaching a single listener to a parent element.

What is the difference between event.target and event.currentTarget?

1. `event.target` is the element where the event listener is attached; `event.currentTarget` is the clicked element.

2. `event.target` is the clicked element; `event.currentTarget` is the element where the event listener is attached.

3. `event.target` and `event.currentTarget` always refer to the same element.

4. `event.target` refers to the parent; `event.currentTarget` refers to the child.

Answer: 2. `event.target` is the clicked element; `event.currentTarget` is the element where the event listener is attached.
Explanation: The `target` is the element that triggered the event, while `currentTarget` is the element to which the event listener is attached.

What does this code do when a <li> inside the list is clicked?

```
document.querySelector("#list").addEventLis
tener("click", (event) => {
  if (event.target.tagName === "LI") {
    console.log("List item clicked!");
  }
});
```

1. Logs "List item clicked!" for any click inside the list.

2. Logs "List item clicked!" only when an `<li>` is clicked.
3. Prevents all clicks on the list.
4. Logs nothing.

Answer: 2. Logs "List item clicked!" only when an `<li>` is clicked.

Explanation: The `if` condition ensures that the message is logged only for `<li>` elements, leveraging event delegation.

What happens if stopPropagation() is called inside an event listener?

1. The event handler executes and the event continues propagating.
2. The event handler executes but prevents further propagation.
3. The event is canceled entirely.
4. All event listeners are removed.

Answer: 2. The event handler executes but prevents further propagation.

Explanation: The `stopPropagation` method allows the current listener to execute but stops the event from propagating to other listeners.

What does this code output when clicking the child element?

```
document.querySelector("#parent").addEventL
istener("click", () => {
  console.log("Parent clicked!");
});
document.querySelector("#child").addEventLi
stener("click", (event) => {
  event.stopPropagation();
  console.log("Child clicked!");
});
```

1. Parent clicked! → Child clicked!
2. Child clicked! → Parent clicked!
3. Only Parent clicked!
4. Only Child clicked!

Answer: 4. Only Child clicked!
Explanation: The stopPropagation method prevents the event from propagating to the parent listener.

Which phase does event.currentTarget reference in?
1. Capturing phase
2. Bubbling phase
3. Both capturing and bubbling phases
4. None

Answer: 3. Both capturing and bubbling phases
Explanation: The currentTarget property is valid in both capturing and bubbling phases because it refers to the element where the listener is attached.

What does the matches method do in the context of event delegation?
1. Checks if an event target matches a specified CSS selector.
2. Prevents an event from propagating to parent elements.
3. Adds a listener to all child elements of a parent.
4. Removes all child elements that match a selector.

Answer: 1. Checks if an event target matches a specified CSS selector.
Explanation: The matches method determines if the target element satisfies a given CSS selector.

Which of the following is true about capturing and bubbling phases?
1. Capturing happens after bubbling.
2. Bubbling happens before capturing.

3. Capturing and bubbling occur simultaneously.
4. Capturing happens before bubbling.

Answer: 4. Capturing happens before bubbling.
Explanation: The capturing phase occurs as the event travels from the root to the target, followed by the bubbling phase as it travels back up.

What does this code output when clicking an <li> element?

```
document.querySelector("#list").addEventLis
tener("click", (event) => {
  console.log(event.target.textContent);
});
```

1. Logs the text content of the clicked <li> element.
2. Logs the text content of the parent <ul> element.
3. Logs nothing.
4. Throws an error.

Answer: 1. Logs the text content of the clicked <li> element.
Explanation: The event.target refers to the element that triggered the event, in this case, the clicked <li>.

What is a key advantage of using event delegation?

1. Prevents event propagation automatically.
2. Reduces the number of event listeners in the DOM.
3. Always executes during the capturing phase.
4. Prevents default browser actions.

Answer: 2. Reduces the number of event listeners in the DOM.
Explanation: Event delegation uses a single listener for multiple child elements, improving performance.

What does this code do?

```
document.body.addEventListener("click",
(event) => {
```

```
if (event.target.tagName === "BUTTON") {
    console.log("Button clicked!");
  }
});
```

1. Executes for all clicks on the document body.
2. Executes only when a button is clicked.
3. Prevents all clicks on buttons.
4. Throws an error if no buttons are clicked.

Answer: 2. Executes only when a button is clicked.
Explanation: The `if` condition ensures the handler executes only for BUTTON elements.

What happens if you attach an event listener to a parent element without using event delegation?

1. The listener handles events for all child elements.
2. Each child element requires its own listener.
3. The event propagation is automatically stopped.
4. The event fires only during the capturing phase.

Answer: 2. Each child element requires its own listener.
Explanation: Without event delegation, individual listeners must be attached to each child element.

What does this code output when clicking an element inside #parent?

```
document.querySelector("#parent").addEventL
istener(
  "click",
  () => {
    console.log("Parent capturing!");
  },
  true
);
```

```
document.querySelector("#child").addEventLi
stener("click", () => {
  console.log("Child bubbling!");
});
```

1. Parent capturing! → Child bubbling!
2. Child bubbling! → Parent capturing!
3. Only Parent capturing!
4. Only Child bubbling!

Answer: 1. Parent capturing! → Child bubbling!
Explanation: The parent listener executes first in the capturing phase, followed by the child listener in the bubbling phase.

Which method ensures that an event listener executes only once?

1. addEventListener(event, handler, { once: true })
2. addEventListener(event, handler, { capture: true })
3. removeEventListener(event, handler)
4. stopImmediatePropagation()

Answer: 1. addEventListener(event, handler, { once: true })
Explanation: The once option ensures the listener is automatically removed after executing once.

What does this code output when clicking a child element?

```
document.querySelector("#parent").addEventL
istener("click", () => {
  console.log("Parent clicked!");
});
```

```
document.querySelector("#child").addEventLi
stener("click", (event) => {
  console.log("Child clicked!");
  event.stopImmediatePropagation();
});
```

1. Parent clicked! → Child clicked!
2. Only Child clicked!
3. Only Parent clicked!
4. Logs nothing.

Answer: 2. Only Child clicked!
Explanation: stopImmediatePropagation prevents the event from propagating to other listeners.

What does this code do?

```
document.querySelector("#container").addEve
ntListener("click", (event) => {
  if
(event.target.classList.contains("btn")) {
    console.log("Button clicked!");
  }
});
```

1. Executes for all clicks inside #container.
2. Executes only when an element with the btn class is clicked.
3. Prevents all clicks on elements inside #container.
4. Logs nothing.

Answer: 2. Executes only when an element with the btn class is clicked.
Explanation: The if condition ensures the listener handles only clicks on elements with the btn class.

try...catch Statements in JavaScript

In JavaScript, the `try...catch` statement is used to handle errors gracefully. Instead of stopping the execution of your code when an error occurs, it allows you to "catch" the error and execute alternative code to handle it. This is especially useful for debugging and building resilient applications.

1. Syntax of try...catch

```
try {
  // Code that may throw an error
} catch (error) {
  // Code to handle the error
}
```

- **try block**: Contains code that might throw an error.
- **catch block**: Executes if an error occurs in the `try` block. It receives an `error` object with details about the error.

Example:

```
try {
  const result = 10 / 0; // No error here
  console.log(result);
} catch (error) {
  console.log("An error occurred:", error.message);
}
```

2. Using finally with try...catch

The `finally` block contains code that will always execute, regardless of whether an error was thrown or not. It's typically used for cleanup actions.

Example:

```
try {
  console.log("Trying...");
} catch (error) {
  console.log("Error caught:",
error.message);
} finally {
  console.log("Execution completed.");
}
```

Output:

```
Trying...
Execution completed.
```

3. Throwing Custom Errors

The throw statement allows you to manually throw an error.

Example:

```
try {
  throw new Error("This is a custom
error.");
} catch (error) {
  console.log("Caught:", error.message);
}
```

4. Nested try...catch

You can nest try...catch statements for handling specific errors separately.

Example:

```
try {
  try {
    JSON.parse("{ invalid: json }");
```

```
} catch (innerError) {
    console.log("Inner error caught:",
innerError.message);
    }
} catch (outerError) {
  console.log("Outer error caught:",
outerError.message);
  }
```

5. Key Properties of the Error Object

- **message**: The error message.
- **name**: The type of error (e.g., TypeError, SyntaxError).
- **stack**: The stack trace (useful for debugging).

Example:

```
try {
  null.method();
} catch (error) {
  console.log("Error name:", error.name);
  console.log("Error message:",
error.message);
  }
```

Multiple-Choice Questions

What is the purpose of the try block?
1. To catch and handle errors.
2. To execute code that may throw an error.
3. To always execute cleanup code.
4. To stop code execution when an error occurs.

Answer: 2. To execute code that may throw an error.
Explanation: The try block contains code that might throw an error.

What happens if no error occurs in the try block?
1. The catch block executes.
2. The catch block is skipped.
3. The finally block is skipped.
4. An error is thrown automatically.

Answer: 2. The catch block is skipped.
Explanation: The catch block only executes if an error occurs in the try block.

What is the purpose of the catch block?
1. To execute code after the try block.
2. To handle errors thrown in the try block.
3. To throw errors manually.
4. To skip error handling.

Answer: 2. To handle errors thrown in the try block.
Explanation: The catch block executes when an error occurs in the try block.

What does this code do?
```
try {
  console.log(variable);
} catch (error) {
  console.log("Error caught:",
error.message);
}
```
1. Logs the value of variable.
2. Logs "Error caught: variable is not defined".
3. Throws an error and stops execution.

4. Skips the catch block.

Answer: 2. Logs "Error caught: variable is not defined".
Explanation: The try block throws a ReferenceError because variable is not defined.

What is the purpose of the finally block?

1. To execute only if an error occurs.
2. To execute code regardless of whether an error occurred or not.
3. To stop the execution of the program.
4. To handle specific types of errors.

Answer: 2. To execute code regardless of whether an error occurred or not.
Explanation: The finally block always executes after the try and catch blocks.

What does this code do?

```
try {
    console.log("Inside try");
} finally {
    console.log("Inside finally");
}
```

1. Logs "Inside try" only.
2. Logs "Inside finally" only.
3. Logs "Inside try" followed by "Inside finally".
4. Throws an error.

Answer: 3. Logs "Inside try" followed by "Inside finally".
Explanation: The finally block always executes, even if no error occurs.

What happens if there is no catch block after a try?
1. The program throws an error.
2. The program skips error handling.
3. The program executes the `finally` block if it exists.
4. The program terminates.

Answer: 3. The program executes the `finally` block if it exists.

Explanation: The `finally` block executes regardless of whether a `catch` block is present.

Which of the following statements throws a custom error?
1. `throw new Error("Custom error");`
2. `console.error("Custom error");`
3. `console.log("Custom error");`
4. `return "Custom error";`

Answer: 1. `throw new Error("Custom error");`

Explanation: The `throw` statement explicitly raises a custom error.

What does this code output?

```
try {
    throw new Error("Something went wrong");
} catch (error) {
    console.log(error.message);
}
```

1. `"Error"`
2. `"Something went wrong"`
3. `undefined`
4. `"error.message"`

Answer: 2. `"Something went wrong"`
Explanation: The `message` property of the `Error` object contains the error message.

What is the role of the Error object in JavaScript?
1. To log errors to the console.
2. To represent an error, including its name and message.
3. To terminate the program.
4. To prevent errors from occurring.

Answer: 2. To represent an error, including its name and message.
Explanation: The `Error` object encapsulates details about an error, such as its name and message.

What does this code do when executed?
```
try {
  JSON.parse("{ invalid: json }");
} catch (error) {
  console.log("Error caught:", error.name);
}
```
1. Logs `Error caught: SyntaxError`.
2. Logs `Error caught: TypeError`.
3. Logs `Error caught: ReferenceError`.
4. Throws an error without logging anything.

Answer: 1. Logs `Error caught: SyntaxError`.
Explanation: The `JSON.parse` method throws a `SyntaxError` when the input string is invalid JSON.

Which block always executes, regardless of whether an error occurs?
1. `try`
2. `catch`

3. `finally`
4. None of the above

Answer: 3. `finally`

Explanation: The `finally` block executes regardless of whether an error is thrown or caught.

What happens if a throw statement is used inside a try block?

1. It skips the `try` block entirely.
2. It triggers the `catch` block.
3. It stops execution without any error handling.
4. It logs the error to the console by default.

Answer: 2. It triggers the `catch` block.

Explanation: The `catch` block is executed when an error is explicitly thrown using the `throw` statement.

What does this code output?

```
try {
  let result = 10 / 0;
  console.log(result);
} catch (error) {
  console.log("Error caught:",
error.message);
}
```

1. Logs `Infinity`.
2. Logs `Error caught: Division by zero`.
3. Throws an error and stops execution.
4. Logs NaN.

Answer: 1. Logs `Infinity`.

Explanation: Division by zero does not throw an error in JavaScript; it returns `Infinity`.

What happens if an error occurs in the catch block?
1. It is ignored and the program continues.
2. It is caught by the same `catch` block.
3. It can be caught by an outer `try...catch`.
4. The program terminates immediately.

Answer: 3. It can be caught by an outer `try...catch`.
Explanation: Errors in the `catch` block can be handled by an outer `try...catch` if it exists.

What does the name property of an error object represent?
1. The type of error (e.g., `SyntaxError`, `TypeError`).
2. The error message.
3. The line number where the error occurred.
4. A custom identifier for the error.

Answer: 1. The type of error (e.g., `SyntaxError`, `TypeError`).
Explanation: The name property specifies the type of error.

What is the output of this code?
```
try {
    throw { name: "CustomError", message:
"This is a custom error" };
} catch (error) {
    console.log(error.name, error.message);
}
```
1. "CustomError: This is a custom error"
2. "Error: This is a custom error"
3. "CustomError This is a custom error"
4. undefined undefined

Answer: 3. `"CustomError This is a custom error"`
Explanation: The thrown object has name and `message` properties, which are accessed in the `catch` block.

What does this code do?
```
try {
  let result = 10 / "a";
  console.log(result);
} catch (error) {
  console.log("Error caught:",
error.message);
}
```
1. Logs NaN.
2. Logs `Error caught: Division by non-numeric value.`
3. Logs `undefined`.
4. Throws a `TypeError`.

Answer: 1. Logs NaN.
Explanation: Dividing a number by a non-numeric string does not throw an error but results in NaN.

What happens if a try block does not throw any error?
1. The `catch` block executes.
2. The `finally` block executes.
3. Both `catch` and `finally` blocks execute.
4. The program skips both `catch` and `finally`.

Answer: 2. The `finally` block executes.
Explanation: The `finally` block always executes, even if no error is thrown in the `try` block.

What is the output of this code?

```
try {
    console.log("Inside try");
    throw new Error("An error occurred");
} catch (error) {
    console.log("Caught:", error.message);
} finally {
    console.log("Finally block executed");
}
```

1. Logs "Inside try" → "Caught: An error occurred" → "Finally block executed".
2. Logs "Inside try" → "Finally block executed" → "Caught: An error occurred".
3. Throws an error and stops execution.
4. Logs "Finally block executed" only.

Answer: 1. Logs "Inside try" → "Caught: An error occurred" → "Finally block executed".
Explanation: The finally block executes after the catch block, even when an error occurs.

What happens if a finally block contains a return statement?

1. It overrides the return statement in the try or catch block.
2. It throws an error.
3. It skips the execution of the finally block.
4. It executes after the try or catch block but before returning.

Answer: 1. It overrides the return statement in the try or catch block.

Explanation: A return in the finally block takes precedence over a return in the try or catch.

Can you have a try block without a catch or finally block?

1. Yes, it's valid.
2. No, a catch or finally block is required.
3. Only if there is no error in the try block.
4. Only if there is a throw statement inside the try block.

Answer: 2. No, a catch or finally block is required.
Explanation: A try block must be followed by either a catch block, a finally block, or both.

What does this code output when an error occurs in the try block?

```
try {
    throw new Error("Test error");
} finally {
    console.log("Finally block executed");
}
```

1. Logs "Finally block executed" only.
2. Logs "Test error" only.
3. Logs "Finally block executed" and rethrows the error.
4. Throws an error without logging anything.

Answer: 3. Logs "Finally block executed" and rethrows the error.
Explanation: The finally block executes, and the error is rethrown if not caught.

What is the best use case for a finally block?

1. Handling errors.

2. Cleaning up resources.
3. Throwing custom errors.
4. Preventing default browser actions.

Answer: 2. Cleaning up resources.
Explanation: The `finally` block is ideal for cleanup actions, such as closing files or releasing locks.

What does this code do when executed?

```
try {
    console.log("No errors here!");
} finally {
    console.log("Finally block executed!");
}
```

1. Logs `"No errors here!"` only.
2. Logs `"Finally block executed!"` only.
3. Logs `"No errors here!"` → `"Finally block executed!"`.
4. Throws an error.

Answer: 3. Logs `"No errors here!"` → `"Finally block executed!"`.
Explanation: The `finally` block executes regardless of whether an error occurs in the `try` block.

Custom Error Messages in JavaScript

JavaScript provides the ability to create and throw custom error messages to make debugging and error handling more meaningful. Custom errors allow developers to provide specific, descriptive error information when something unexpected happens in the code.

1. Throwing Custom Errors

You can use the `throw` statement to raise an error, which can be a JavaScript `Error` object or any value (though using `Error` objects is recommended).

Example: Throwing a Custom Error

```
function divide(a, b) {
  if (b === 0) {
    throw new Error("Division by zero is
not allowed.");
  }
  return a / b;
}
try {
  console.log(divide(10, 0));
} catch (error) {
  console.log("Error:", error.message); //
Logs "Division by zero is not allowed."
}
```

2. The Error Object

The `Error` object provides important information about the error:

- **message**: A string describing the error.
- **name**: The type of error (e.g., `Error`, `TypeError`).
- **stack**: A stack trace showing where the error occurred.

Example: Using the Error Object

```
try {
  throw new Error("Custom error message");
} catch (error) {
  console.log(error.name); // Logs "Error"
```

```
  console.log(error.message); // Logs
"Custom error message"
}
```

3. Custom Error Classes

You can define custom error types by extending the `Error` class.

Example: Custom Error Class

```
class ValidationError extends Error {
  constructor(message) {
    super(message);
    this.name = "ValidationError";
  }
}
try {
  throw new ValidationError("Invalid input
provided");
} catch (error) {
  console.log(`${error.name}:
${error.message}`); // Logs
"ValidationError: Invalid input provided"
}
```

4. Benefits of Custom Errors

- **Improved Debugging**: Provides more context about the error.
- **Standardization**: Makes error handling consistent.
- **Separation of Concerns**: Different error types for different issues.

5. Key Points for Throwing Custom Errors

- Always use the Error object or its subclasses for throwing errors.
- Include meaningful message values to help identify the issue.
- Use try...catch to handle errors where needed.

Multiple-Choice Questions

What is the purpose of throwing custom errors?

1. To stop program execution entirely.
2. To provide more descriptive and meaningful error messages.
3. To replace all existing error handling mechanisms.
4. To prevent errors from occurring.

Answer: 2. To provide more descriptive and meaningful error messages.

Explanation: Custom errors allow developers to convey specific details about the problem, improving debugging and user experience.

Which statement correctly throws a custom error?

1. ```
   throw "Custom error";
   ```
2. ```
   throw new Error("Custom error
   message");
   ```
3. ```
   throw Error("Custom error message");
   ```
4. All of the above

Answer: 4. All of the above

Explanation: Errors can be thrown as strings or Error objects, but using Error objects is the recommended approach.

What is the output of this code?

```
try {
```
```

```
    throw new Error("An error occurred");
} catch (error) {
    console.log(error.message);
}
```

1. "Error: An error occurred"
2. "An error occurred"
3. undefined
4. null

Answer: 2. "An error occurred"
Explanation: The message property of the Error object contains the error description.

Which property of the Error object contains the stack trace?

1. message
2. name
3. stack
4. trace

Answer: 3. stack
Explanation: The stack property provides a stack trace, which is useful for debugging.

How do you create a custom error class?

1. By inheriting from the Error class.
2. By creating a regular JavaScript class.
3. By overriding the throw statement.
4. By redefining the Error object.

Answer: 1. By inheriting from the Error class.
Explanation: A custom error class is created by extending the Error class and optionally adding custom properties or methods.

What does this code output?

```
class CustomError extends Error {
  constructor(message) {
    super(message);
    this.name = "CustomError";
  }
}
try {
  throw new CustomError("This is a custom
error.");
} catch (error) {
  console.log(error.name, error.message);
}
```

1. "Error: This is a custom error."
2. "CustomError This is a custom error."
3. "Error CustomError"
4. undefined undefined

Answer: 2. "CustomError This is a custom
error."
Explanation: The name property is set to
"CustomError", and the message contains the custom
error message.

Which method ensures that a thrown error is logged
with a custom message?

1. `console.log("Error:", error);`
2. `throw new Error("Custom error
   message");`
3. `console.error("Custom error:",
   error.message);`
4. All of the above

Answer: 4. All of the above
Explanation: All these methods can be used to provide more context when logging or throwing errors.

What does this code output?

```
try {
    throw new TypeError("This is a type
error.");
} catch (error) {
    console.log(error.name, error.message);
}
```

1. "TypeError: This is a type error."
2. "TypeError This is a type error."
3. "Error This is a type error."
4. undefined undefined

Answer: 2. "TypeError This is a type error."
Explanation: The name property is "TypeError", and the message contains the custom error message.

What is the output of this code?

```
try {
    throw { message: "Custom object error",
code: 404 };
} catch (error) {
    console.log(error.message, error.code);
}
```

1. "Custom object error"
2. "Custom object error 404"
3. "404 Custom object error"
4. Throws an error

Answer: 2. `"Custom object error 404"`
Explanation: The `throw` statement can raise any value, and its properties are accessible in the `catch` block.

What is the recommended approach for throwing errors in JavaScript?
1. Using strings directly.
2. Using `Error` objects or their subclasses.
3. Using anonymous functions.
4. Using global variables.

Answer: 2. Using `Error` objects or their subclasses.
Explanation: Using `Error` objects ensures consistency and provides useful debugging information like stack traces.

What is the output of this code?
```
try {
    throw new SyntaxError("Invalid syntax.");
} catch (error) {
    console.log(error.name, error.message);
}
```
1. `"Error Invalid syntax."`
2. `"SyntaxError Invalid syntax."`
3. `"TypeError Invalid syntax."`
4. `undefined undefined`

Answer: 2. `"SyntaxError Invalid syntax."`
Explanation: The name property is `"SyntaxError"`, and the `message` contains the custom error description.

Which of the following is true about the message property of an Error object?
1. It is required when throwing an error.
2. It provides details about the error.

3. It contains the stack trace.
4. It is automatically set to "Error" if omitted.

Answer: 2. It provides details about the error.
Explanation: The message property describes the error and is optional but recommended for clarity.

What happens if you call throw without specifying a value?
1. It throws undefined.
2. It throws an empty Error object.
3. It throws null.
4. It throws a default error message.

Answer: 1. It throws undefined.
Explanation: The throw statement requires a value, but if none is provided, it throws undefined.

What does this code do?
```
try {
    throw new Error();
} catch (error) {
    console.log(error.message);
}
```
1. Logs "Error"
2. Logs an empty string
3. Logs "undefined"
4. Throws an error

Answer: 2. Logs an empty string
Explanation: If no message is provided when creating an Error object, the message property defaults to an empty string.

What is the purpose of the name property in a custom error class?

1. To store the name of the developer.
2. To differentiate custom errors from other error types.
3. To provide additional error messages.
4. To track the error's location in the code.

Answer: 2. To differentiate custom errors from other error types.

Explanation: The name property specifies the type of error, making it easier to identify in error handling.

What does this code output?

```
class DatabaseError extends Error {
  constructor(message) {
    super(message);
    this.name = "DatabaseError";
  }
}
try {
  throw new DatabaseError("Failed to
connect to database.");
} catch (error) {
  console.log(`${error.name}:
${error.message}`);
}
```

1. "Error: Failed to connect to database."
2. "DatabaseError: Failed to connect to database."
3. "TypeError: Failed to connect to database."
4. Throws an error

Answer: 2. `"DatabaseError: Failed to connect to database."`
Explanation: The custom error class sets the name to `"DatabaseError"`, and the `message` contains the error description.

What is a benefit of using custom error classes in JavaScript?

1. They automatically fix errors.
2. They allow for more specific error handling.
3. They make code execution faster.
4. They prevent exceptions from being thrown.

Answer: 2. They allow for more specific error handling.
Explanation: Custom error classes make it easier to identify and handle specific types of errors in large applications.

What happens if you throw an error object that lacks a name property?

1. It defaults to `"Error"`.
2. It throws an exception.
3. It sets the name to `"UnknownError"`.
4. The error is ignored.

Answer: 1. It defaults to `"Error"`.
Explanation: The `Error` class automatically sets the name property to `"Error"` if not explicitly defined.

What is the output of this code?

```
try {
    throw { code: 500, message: "Internal
Server Error" };
} catch (error) {
    console.log(error.code, error.message);
}
```

1. "500 Internal Server Error"
2. 500 "Internal Server Error"
3. "Internal Server Error 500"
4. undefined undefined

Answer: 2. 500 "Internal Server Error"
Explanation: The thrown object's code and message properties are accessible in the catch block.

What is the difference between throw new Error("Message") and throw "Message"?

1. The first creates an Error object, while the second throws a string.
2. The second is invalid syntax.
3. Both create identical error messages.
4. The first only works with custom error classes.

Answer: 1. The first creates an Error object, while the second throws a string.
Explanation: Throwing an Error object provides more information (e.g., stack trace) compared to a string.

Which property is automatically set when an Error object is created?

1. name
2. message
3. stack
4. All of the above

Answer: 4. All of the above
Explanation: The Error object automatically sets the name, message, and stack properties.

What happens if a thrown error is not caught by a try...catch block?

1. It is ignored.
2. It terminates the program.

3. It bubbles up the call stack.
4. It logs a warning to the console.

Answer: 3. It bubbles up the call stack.
Explanation: Uncaught errors propagate up the call stack, potentially terminating the program if unhandled.

What is the best practice for creating meaningful custom error messages?
1. Use detailed, descriptive messages.
2. Avoid using the `Error` object.
3. Only use string literals.
4. Include irrelevant information for debugging.

Answer: 1. Use detailed, descriptive messages.
Explanation: Detailed messages make it easier to understand and fix errors during debugging.

What is the default value of the message property when creating an Error object without arguments?
1. `"Error occurred"`
2. `" "` (empty string)
3. `undefined`
4. `"No message provided"`

Answer: 2. `" "` (empty string)
Explanation: If no message is provided, the `message` property defaults to an empty string.

What does this code output?

```
try {
  throw new Error("Custom error example");
} catch (error) {
  console.log(error.stack);
}
```

1. The error's stack trace.
2. `"Custom error example"`

3. undefined

4. Throws an error

Answer: 1. The error's stack trace.

Explanation: The `stack` property contains the stack trace, showing where the error occurred.

Let me know if you need further clarification or assistance!

setTimeout and setInterval in JavaScript

JavaScript provides two key functions for scheduling code execution: **setTimeout** and **setInterval**. These functions are used to execute code after a delay or at regular intervals.

1. setTimeout

The `setTimeout` function executes a piece of code or function after a specified delay (in milliseconds).

Syntax:

```
const timeoutId = setTimeout(callback,
delay, arg1, arg2, ...);
```

- **callback**: The function to execute after the delay.

- **delay**: Time in milliseconds to wait before executing the function.

- **Optional arguments (arg1, arg2, ...)**: Arguments passed to the callback function.

Example:

```
setTimeout(() => {
  console.log("This message appears after 2 seconds.");
}, 2000);
```

2. setInterval

The `setInterval` function repeatedly executes a piece of code or function at a fixed time interval.

Syntax:

```
const intervalId = setInterval(callback,
delay, arg1, arg2, ...);
```

- **callback**: The function to execute at each interval.
- **delay**: Time in milliseconds between each function execution.

Example:

```
const intervalId = setInterval(() => {
  console.log("This message appears every second.");
}, 1000);
```

3. Clearing Timers

Both `setTimeout` and `setInterval` return a timer ID. Use this ID to clear the timer when needed.

3.1. clearTimeout

Stops a timer set with `setTimeout`.

Example:

```
const timeoutId = setTimeout(() => {
  console.log("This will not run.");
}, 5000);
clearTimeout(timeoutId);
```

3.2. clearInterval

Stops a timer set with `setInterval`.

Example:

```
const intervalId = setInterval(() => {
  console.log("Repeating...");
```

```
}, 1000);
setTimeout(() => {
  clearInterval(intervalId);
  console.log("Interval cleared.");
}, 5000);
```

4. Key Points

- Timers are asynchronous and do not block code execution.
- The actual delay may vary due to JavaScript's single-threaded nature and event loop.
- Use clearTimeout and clearInterval to prevent timers from running indefinitely or executing unnecessarily.

Multiple-Choice Questions

What does setTimeout do?
1. Executes a function immediately.
2. Executes a function after a specified delay.
3. Executes a function repeatedly at fixed intervals.
4. Stops a previously set timer.

Answer: 2. Executes a function after a specified delay.
Explanation: The setTimeout function schedules a one-time execution of a callback after a delay.

What does setInterval do?
1. Executes a function after a delay.
2. Executes a function repeatedly at fixed intervals.
3. Stops an ongoing timer.
4. Immediately clears all timers.

Answer: 2. Executes a function repeatedly at fixed intervals.

Explanation: The `setInterval` function executes a callback repeatedly at the specified interval.

What does clearTimeout do?
1. Clears a timer set by `setTimeout`.
2. Clears a timer set by `setInterval`.
3. Stops all running timers.
4. Resets the execution context.

Answer: 1. Clears a timer set by `setTimeout`.
Explanation: The `clearTimeout` function stops the execution of a timer set by `setTimeout`.

What does this code do?
```
setTimeout(() => {
  console.log("Hello!");
}, 3000);
```
1. Logs "`Hello!`" immediately.
2. Logs "`Hello!`" after 3 seconds.
3. Logs "`Hello!`" every 3 seconds.
4. Does nothing.

Answer: 2. Logs "`Hello!`" after 3 seconds.
Explanation: The `setTimeout` function delays the execution of the callback by 3 seconds.

How do you stop a repeating timer set with setInterval?
1. `clearTimeout(timerId)`
2. `clearInterval(timerId)`
3. `stopTimer(timerId)`
4. `stopInterval(timerId)`

Answer: 2. `clearInterval(timerId)`
Explanation: The `clearInterval` function stops a timer set with `setInterval`.

What is the output of this code?

```
let count = 0;
const intervalId = setInterval(() => {
  console.log(++count);
  if (count === 3) {
    clearInterval(intervalId);
  }
}, 1000);
```

  1. Logs 1 2 3 at 1-second intervals, then stops.
  2. Logs 1 2 3 immediately, then stops.
  3. Runs indefinitely without stopping.
  4. Throws an error.

Answer: 1. Logs 1 2 3 at 1-second intervals, then stops.
Explanation: The clearInterval function stops the timer when count reaches 3.

What does this code do?

```
const timeoutId = setTimeout(() => {
  console.log("Executed after 5 seconds.");
}, 5000);
clearTimeout(timeoutId);
```

  1. Executes the callback after 5 seconds.
  2. Executes the callback immediately.
  3. Prevents the callback from executing.
  4. Throws an error.

Answer: 3. Prevents the callback from executing.
Explanation: The clearTimeout function cancels the timer, so the callback is never executed.

Which of the following is true about setTimeout?

  1. It blocks code execution until the delay is over.
  2. It is synchronous.

3. It is asynchronous.
4. It requires `clearTimeout` to run.

Answer: 3. It is asynchronous.
Explanation: The `setTimeout` function schedules the callback asynchronously, allowing other code to execute during the delay.

What happens if setInterval is called with a delay of 0?
1. Executes the callback immediately.
2. Executes the callback as soon as possible after the current task.
3. Executes the callback only once.
4. Throws an error.

Answer: 2. Executes the callback as soon as possible after the current task.
Explanation: A `setInterval` with 0 delay runs the callback after the current execution stack is cleared.

What does this code do?
```
setTimeout(console.log, 2000, "Delayed
message");
```
1. Throws an error.
2. Logs "Delayed message" immediately.
3. Logs "Delayed message" after 2 seconds.
4. Does nothing.

Answer: 3. Logs "Delayed message" after 2 seconds.
Explanation: The third argument of `setTimeout` is passed as an argument to the callback function.

What is the difference between setTimeout and setInterval?
1. `setTimeout` executes a function once; `setInterval` executes it repeatedly.
2. `setTimeout` is synchronous; `setInterval` is asynchronous.

3. `setTimeout` blocks the thread; `setInterval` does not.
4. There is no difference.

Answer: 1. `setTimeout` executes a function once; `setInterval` executes it repeatedly.

Explanation: The `setTimeout` function schedules a one-time execution, while `setInterval` schedules repeated executions.

What is returned by setTimeout or setInterval?
1. A promise.
2. A timer ID.
3. The result of the callback function.
4. `undefined`.

Answer: 2. A timer ID.

Explanation: Both `setTimeout` and `setInterval` return a timer ID, which can be used to cancel the timer with `clearTimeout` or `clearInterval`.

What does this code output?

```
setTimeout(() => {
  console.log("First");
}, 0);
console.log("Second");
```

1. `"First"` followed by `"Second"`.
2. `"Second"` followed by `"First"`.
3. `"First"` only.
4. `"Second"` only.

Answer: 2. `"Second"` followed by `"First"`.

Explanation: Even with a delay of 0, the `setTimeout` callback is executed after the current task completes, making it asynchronous.

What happens if clearTimeout is called with an invalid timer ID?

1. It throws an error.
2. It cancels all timers.
3. It does nothing.
4. It logs a warning.

Answer: 3. It does nothing.
Explanation: Calling `clearTimeout` with an invalid ID has no effect and does not throw an error.

How can you pass arguments to a callback function used in setTimeout?

1. By defining them in the `setTimeout` call after the delay.
2. By defining them as global variables.
3. By returning the arguments from the callback.
4. By wrapping the callback in an anonymous function.

Answer: 1. By defining them in the `setTimeout` call after the delay.
Explanation: Arguments passed after the delay are passed to the callback when it is executed.
Example:

```
setTimeout((name) => {
  console.log(`Hello, ${name}`);
}, 1000, "Alice"); // Logs "Hello, Alice"
after 1 second.
```

Which of the following will stop a timer set by setInterval?

1. `clearTimeout(timerId)`
2. `clearInterval(timerId)`
3. `stopInterval(timerId)`
4. `terminateTimer(timerId)`

Answer: 2. `clearInterval(timerId)`
Explanation: The `clearInterval` function stops a timer set by `setInterval`.

What does this code do?
```
let counter = 0;
const intervalId = setInterval(() => {
  console.log(++counter);
  if (counter === 5) {
    clearInterval(intervalId);
  }
}, 1000);
```
1. Logs numbers 1 to 5 every second, then stops.
2. Logs numbers indefinitely.
3. Throws an error.
4. Logs numbers 1 to 5 immediately.

Answer: 1. Logs numbers 1 to 5 every second, then stops.
Explanation: The `clearInterval` function stops the timer when the condition is met.

What is the behavior of setTimeout when used inside a loop?
1. Executes all iterations immediately.
2. Executes each callback sequentially after the delay.
3. Executes all callbacks after the loop completes.
4. Executes callbacks asynchronously, based on the loop's behavior.

Answer: 4. Executes callbacks asynchronously, based on the loop's behavior.
Explanation: The `setTimeout` callbacks are scheduled for execution asynchronously, and their behavior depends on closures and the loop.

What does this code output?

```
for (let i = 1; i <= 3; i++) {
  setTimeout(() => {
    console.log(i);
  }, i * 1000);
}
```

1. Logs 1 2 3 immediately.
2. Logs 1 after 1 second, 2 after 2 seconds, 3 after 3 seconds.
3. Logs 3 three times after 3 seconds.
4. Throws an error.

Answer: 2. Logs 1 after 1 second, 2 after 2 seconds, 3 after 3 seconds.
Explanation: The `let` keyword ensures a new scope for each iteration, so the correct value of i is captured in the closure.

What happens if setTimeout is called with a negative delay?

1. The callback executes immediately.
2. The callback executes after a default delay of 0.
3. The callback does not execute.
4. Throws an error.

Answer: 1. The callback executes immediately.
Explanation: Negative or zero delays are treated as 0, and the callback is scheduled for immediate execution after the current task.

Which of the following correctly stops an ongoing setInterval?

1. `clearInterval()` without arguments.
2. `clearInterval()` with a valid timer ID.
3. `stopTimer(timerId)`

4. `terminateInterval(timerId)`

Answer: 2. `clearInterval()` with a valid timer ID.
Explanation: The `clearInterval` function requires a valid timer ID to stop the interval.

What does this code output?
```
console.log("Start");
setTimeout(() => {
  console.log("Timeout");
}, 0);
console.log("End");
```
    1. `"Start"` → `"Timeout"` → `"End"`
    2. `"Start"` → `"End"` → `"Timeout"`
    3. `"Timeout"` → `"Start"` → `"End"`
    4. Throws an error.

Answer: 2. `"Start"` → `"End"` → `"Timeout"`
Explanation: The `setTimeout` callback executes after the current execution context finishes, even with a 0 delay.

What is the minimum delay for setTimeout guaranteed by the browser?
    1. 0 ms
    2. 1 ms
    3. 4 ms
    4. 10 ms

Answer: 3. 4 ms
Explanation: The HTML5 specification mandates a minimum delay of 4 ms for `setTimeout` in most modern browsers.

What happens if setInterval is called with a delay of Infinity?
    1. The callback never executes.

2. The callback executes once.
3. The callback executes after the first event loop.
4. Throws an error.

Answer: 1. The callback never executes.
Explanation: A delay of `Infinity` effectively prevents the callback from ever being executed.

Which of the following is true about setTimeout and setInterval?
1. Both are synchronous.
2. Both return a promise.
3. Both are asynchronous and return a timer ID.
4. Both block the main thread until completion.

Answer: 3. Both are asynchronous and return a timer ID.
Explanation: Both functions are asynchronous and return a timer ID that can be used to manage the timer.

Introduction to Callbacks in JavaScript

In JavaScript, **callbacks** are functions passed as arguments to other functions to be executed later. They are a cornerstone of asynchronous programming, enabling you to handle tasks like fetching data, reading files, or responding to user interactions.

1. What is a Callback?

A callback is a function passed to another function as an argument, which is then invoked within the outer function to complete a specific task.

Example:

```
function greet(name, callback) {
  console.log(`Hello, ${name}!`);
  callback();
}
```

```
function sayGoodbye() {
  console.log("Goodbye!");
}
greet("Alice", sayGoodbye);
// Output:
// Hello, Alice!
// Goodbye!
```

2. Synchronous Callbacks

A synchronous callback executes immediately during the execution of the containing function.

Example:

```
function processArray(arr, callback) {
  arr.forEach(callback);
}
processArray([1, 2, 3], (number) => {
  console.log(number * 2);
});
// Output:
// 2
// 4
// 6
```

3. Asynchronous Callbacks

An asynchronous callback is executed later, typically after an operation like fetching data or waiting for a timeout.

Example:

```
setTimeout(() => {
  console.log("This message is delayed by 2 seconds.");
}, 2000);
```

4. Why Use Callbacks?

- **Control Flow**: Callbacks allow you to decide what happens after a certain operation finishes.
- **Reusability**: The same callback can be used in multiple places.
- **Handling Asynchronous Tasks**: Callbacks are essential for tasks like API calls, timers, and event handling.

5. Nested Callbacks and Callback Hell

When callbacks are nested inside one another, the code can become harder to read and maintain, often referred to as **callback hell**.

Example:

```
setTimeout(() => {
  console.log("Step 1");
  setTimeout(() => {
    console.log("Step 2");
    setTimeout(() => {
      console.log("Step 3");
    }, 1000);
  }, 1000);
}, 1000);
```

6. Key Points to Remember

- Callbacks can be synchronous or asynchronous.
- Be cautious of deeply nested callbacks (callback hell) and consider using Promises or async/await for cleaner code.
- Always handle errors in callbacks to prevent unexpected behavior.

Multiple-Choice Questions

What is a callback function?

1. A function that executes immediately after being defined.
2. A function passed as an argument to another function to be executed later.
3. A function that is called at the end of a program.
4. A function that runs synchronously.

Answer: 2. A function passed as an argument to another function to be executed later.

Explanation: A callback is a function provided to another function to control execution flow or handle asynchronous operations.

Which of the following is an example of using a callback function?

1. ```
   function greet()
   {console.log("Hello");}greet();
   ```
2. ```
   function greet(callback) {
   callback();}greet(() =>
   console.log("Hello"));
   ```
3. ```
   console.log("Hello");
   ```
4. None of the above

Answer: 2.

```
function greet(callback) {
  callback();
}
greet(() => console.log("Hello"));
```

Explanation: Here, the function greet takes a callback function as an argument and invokes it.

What does this code output?

```
function process(number, callback) {
```
```

```
  callback(number * 2);
}
process(5, (result) => {
  console.log(result);
});
```

1. 5
2. 10
3. NaN
4. Throws an error

Answer: 2. 10
Explanation: The `process` function passes `number * 2` (10) to the callback, which logs it.

What type of callback is used in this code?

```
setTimeout(() => {
  console.log("Delayed message");
}, 2000);
```

1. Synchronous
2. Asynchronous
3. Blocking
4. Recursive

Answer: 2. Asynchronous
Explanation: The callback is executed after a delay, making it asynchronous.

What does this code output?

```
function greet(name, callback) {
  console.log(`Hello, ${name}!`);
  callback();
}
greet("Alice", () => {
  console.log("Goodbye!");
```

```
});
```

1. Hello, Alice!
   Goodbye!
2. Goodbye!
   Hello, Alice!
3. Hello, Alice! only
4. Throws an error

Answer: 1.

```
Hello, Alice!
Goodbye!
```

Explanation: The `greet` function logs the greeting, then invokes the callback to log the goodbye message.

What is the output of this code?

```
function multiply(x, y, callback) {
  const result = x * y;
  callback(result);
}
multiply(3, 4, (result) => {
  console.log(result);
});
```

1. 7
2. 12
3. Throws an error
4. undefined

Answer: 2. 12

Explanation: The `multiply` function computes x * y (12) and passes it to the callback, which logs it.

What is "callback hell"?

1. A situation where callbacks fail to execute.
2. A series of deeply nested callbacks, making code hard to read.

3. A situation where callbacks run synchronously.
4. A term for an unhandled callback.

Answer: 2. A series of deeply nested callbacks, making code hard to read.
Explanation: Callback hell occurs when multiple nested callbacks make the code complex and difficult to maintain.

What is the best way to handle callback hell?
1. Avoid using callbacks.
2. Use Promises or `async/await`.
3. Nest callbacks deeper.
4. Use global variables instead.

Answer: 2. Use Promises or `async/await`.
Explanation: Promises and `async/await` simplify asynchronous code, avoiding deeply nested callbacks.

What does this code output?

```
function add(a, b, callback) {
    callback(a + b);
}
add(5, 10, (result) => {
    console.log(result * 2);
});
```

1. 15
2. 20
3. 30
4. Throws an error

Answer: 3. 30
Explanation: The add function calculates a + b (15) and passes it to the callback, which multiplies it by 2 and logs 30.

Which of the following is an example of a synchronous callback?

1. ```
   setTimeout(() => {
   console.log("Hello");}, 1000);
   ```
2. ```
   [1, 2, 3].forEach((num) =>
   {  console.log(num);});
   ```
3. ```
   fetch("https://example.com").then((res
   ponse) => console.log(response));
   ```
4. None of the above

Answer: 2.

```
[1, 2, 3].forEach((num) => {
  console.log(num);
});
```

Explanation: The callback in `forEach` is executed immediately and synchronously for each array element.

What is the output of this code?

```
function displayMessage(callback) {
  callback("Welcome to callbacks!");
}
displayMessage((message) => {
  console.log(message);
});
```

1. "Welcome to callbacks!"
2. "Undefined"
3. Throws an error
4. null

Answer: 1. "Welcome to Callbacks!"
Explanation: The `displayMessage` function passes the string to the callback, which logs it.
```

Which of the following scenarios best illustrates a real-world use case for a callback?

1. Printing a message to the console.
2. Fetching data from an API and displaying it after the data is loaded.
3. Adding two numbers and returning the result.
4. Assigning a value to a variable.

Answer: 2. Fetching data from an API and displaying it after the data is loaded.

Explanation: Callbacks are commonly used to handle asynchronous operations like fetching data.

What does this code output?

```
setTimeout(() => {
  console.log("A");
}, 2000);
console.log("B");
```

1. "A" followed by "B"
2. "B" followed by "A"
3. Logs "A" only
4. Throws an error

Answer: 2. "B" followed by "A"

Explanation: The setTimeout callback is executed asynchronously after 2 seconds, so "B" logs first.

What does this code output?

```
function repeat(num, callback) {
  for (let i = 0; i < num; i++) {
    callback(i);
  }
}
repeat(3, (index) => {
  console.log(`Index: ${index}`);
```

```
});
```

1. Logs "Index: 0", "Index: 1", "Index: 2"
2. Logs "Index: 0", "Index: 1"
3. Logs "Index: 0" only
4. Throws an error

Answer: 1. Logs "Index: 0", "Index: 1", "Index: 2"

Explanation: The repeat function invokes the callback for each iteration of the loop, passing the current index.

What is a key advantage of using callbacks?

1. They eliminate errors in the code.
2. They improve performance of synchronous tasks.
3. They allow asynchronous operations to execute in order.
4. They remove the need for loops.

Answer: 3. They allow asynchronous operations to execute in order.

Explanation: Callbacks enable controlled execution of code after an asynchronous operation completes.

What is the output of this code?

```
function fetchData(callback) {
  setTimeout(() => {
    callback("Data loaded");
  }, 1000);
}
fetchData((data) => {
  console.log(data);
});
```

1. Logs "Data loaded" after 1 second.
2. Logs "Data loaded" immediately.
3. Logs "Undefined"

4. Throws an error

Answer: 1. Logs "Data loaded" after 1 second.
Explanation: The callback is executed by setTimeout after the specified delay of 1 second.

What does this code output?

```
function calculate(a, b, callback) {
  const result = a + b;
  callback(result);
}
calculate(2, 3, (sum) => {
  console.log(sum * 2);
});
```

1. 10
2. 6
3. 5
4. Throws an error

Answer: 1. 10
Explanation: The calculate function computes 2 + 3 and passes the result to the callback, which multiplies it by 2 and logs 10.

What does this code illustrate?

```
setTimeout(() => {
  console.log("Step 1");
  setTimeout(() => {
    console.log("Step 2");
    setTimeout(() => {
      console.log("Step 3");
    }, 1000);
  }, 1000);
}, 1000);
```

1. Error handling in callbacks
2. Callback hell
3. Synchronous callback execution
4. Nested promises

Answer: 2. Callback hell

Explanation: The nested `setTimeout` calls create deeply indented and harder-to-read code, a common example of callback hell.

What is the output of this code?

```
[1, 2, 3].forEach((num) => {
  console.log(num * 2);
});
```

1. 1, 2, 3
2. 2, 4, 6
3. 1 2 3
4. Throws an error

Answer: 2. 2, 4, 6

Explanation: The `forEach` method executes the callback for each array element, multiplying each by 2.

What happens if a callback is not passed to a function that requires one?

1. The function throws an error.
2. The function runs without executing the callback.
3. The function stops execution.
4. The function creates a default callback.

Answer: 2. The function runs without executing the callback.

Explanation: If a callback is not provided, the function executes normally but skips the callback invocation.

What is the output of this code?

```
function executeCallback(callback) {
```

```
  console.log("Before callback");
  callback();
  console.log("After callback");
}
executeCallback(() => {
  console.log("Inside callback");
});
```

1. `"Before callback"`, `"After callback"`
2. `"Before callback"`, `"Inside callback"`, `"After callback"`
3. `"Inside callback"` only
4. Throws an error

Answer: 2. `"Before callback"`, `"Inside callback"`, `"After callback"`

Explanation: The executeCallback function logs a message, invokes the callback, and logs another message afterward.

What is the primary difference between synchronous and asynchronous callbacks?

1. Synchronous callbacks are functions, asynchronous callbacks are not.
2. Synchronous callbacks execute immediately, asynchronous callbacks execute later.
3. Asynchronous callbacks cannot use parameters.
4. Synchronous callbacks can only run in loops.

Answer: 2. Synchronous callbacks execute immediately, asynchronous callbacks execute later.

Explanation: Synchronous callbacks are executed during the execution of the function, while asynchronous callbacks are executed after some time or event.

What is the best practice for handling errors in callbacks?

1. Use try-catch blocks inside the callback.
2. Assume no errors will occur.
3. Ignore the callback's behavior.
4. Always use a promise instead.

Answer: 1. Use try-catch blocks inside the callback.
Explanation: Using `try-catch` ensures that errors in the callback are handled properly, preventing unexpected behavior.

What does this code output?

```
function operation(a, b, callback) {
  if (b === 0) {
    callback("Cannot divide by zero",
null);
  } else {
    callback(null, a / b);
  }
}
operation(10, 0, (err, result) => {
  if (err) {
    console.log(err);
  } else {
    console.log(result);
  }
});
```

1. "Cannot divide by zero"
2. 10
3. null
4. Throws an error

Answer: 1. `"Cannot divide by zero"`
Explanation: The function checks if b is 0, and if true, it passes an error message to the callback.

What is the primary benefit of using callbacks?
1. They improve code readability.
2. They enable asynchronous operations.
3. They simplify synchronous tasks.
4. They eliminate the need for loops.

Answer: 2. They enable asynchronous operations.
Explanation: Callbacks are crucial for handling tasks like fetching data or responding to events without blocking the execution of other code.

Arrow Functions in JavaScript

Arrow functions, introduced in ES6 (ECMAScript 2015), provide a concise syntax for writing functions. They are especially useful for shorter functions and callbacks but differ from traditional functions in some key ways.

1. Syntax of Arrow Functions

Basic Syntax:

```
const add = (a, b) => a + b;
```

- **Parameters**: Placed inside parentheses.
- **Arrow (=>)**: Separates the parameters from the function body.
- **Body**: If the body contains a single expression, it can be returned implicitly without `return`.

Examples:

```
// Traditional function
function multiply(a, b) {
  return a * b;
}
```

```
// Arrow function
const multiply = (a, b) => a * b;
console.log(multiply(2, 3)); // Output: 6
```

2. Features of Arrow Functions

2.1. Implicit Return

If the function body has only one expression, you can omit the {} and return.

Example:

```
const square = x => x * x; // Implicit
return
console.log(square(4)); // Output: 16
```

2.2. No this Binding

Arrow functions do not have their own this. They inherit this from the enclosing lexical scope.

Example:

```
function Person(name) {
  this.name = name;
  setTimeout(() => {
    console.log(`Hello, ${this.name}`);
  }, 1000);
}
const john = new Person("John");
// Output: Hello, John
```

3. Differences Between Arrow Functions and Regular Functions

Feature	Arrow Function	Regular Function

this Binding	Inherits this from the enclosing scope.	Has its own this.
arguments Object	Does not have the arguments object.	Has the arguments object.
Use as a Constructor	Cannot be used as a constructor.	Can be used as a constructor.
Syntax	Shorter and more concise.	Longer and more explicit.

4. Common Use Cases

- Short callbacks:

```
const numbers = [1, 2, 3];
const squares = numbers.map(num => num *
num);
console.log(squares); // Output: [1, 4, 9]
```

- Simplifying code readability:

```
const isEven = num => num % 2 === 0;
console.log(isEven(4)); // Output: true
```

Multiple-Choice Questions

What is the correct syntax for an arrow function with two parameters?

1. `const add = (a, b) => a + b;`
2. `const add = (a, b) { a + b };`
3. `function add(a, b) => a + b;`
4. `const add => (a, b) => { return a + b; };`

Answer: 1. `const add = (a, b) => a + b;`
Explanation: Arrow functions use the => syntax and can omit the `return` statement for single-expression bodies.

What does this code output?
```
const greet = () => "Hello, World!";
console.log(greet());
```
    1. `"Hello, World!"`
    2. `undefined`
    3. `null`
    4. Throws an error
Answer: 1. `"Hello, World!"`
Explanation: The arrow function implicitly returns the string `"Hello, World!"`.

What happens if an arrow function is used as a constructor?
    1. It works like a regular function.
    2. It throws an error.
    3. It returns `undefined`.
    4. It creates an object but ignores `this`.
Answer: 2. It throws an error.
Explanation: Arrow functions cannot be used as constructors because they do not have their own `this`.

What is the output of this code?
```
const numbers = [1, 2, 3];
const doubled = numbers.map(num => num * 2);
console.log(doubled);
```
    1. `[2, 4, 6]`
    2. `[1, 4, 9]`
    3. `[1, 2, 3]`

4. Throws an error

Answer: 1. [2, 4, 6]
Explanation: The map method uses the arrow function to double each element of the array.

What does this code output?

```
const add = (a, b) => { return a + b; };
console.log(add(3, 4));
```

1. 7
2. undefined
3. Throws an error
4. null

Answer: 1. 7
Explanation: The arrow function explicitly returns the sum of a and b.

What happens to the this keyword in an arrow function?

1. It binds to the global object.
2. It binds to the enclosing lexical scope.
3. It binds to the function's execution context.
4. It is undefined.

Answer: 2. It binds to the enclosing lexical scope.
Explanation: Arrow functions inherit this from their surrounding context.

Which statement about arrow functions is true?

1. They have an arguments object.
2. They can be used as constructors.
3. They are ideal for methods that use this.
4. They provide a shorter syntax for writing functions.

Answer: 4. They provide a shorter syntax for writing functions.

Explanation: Arrow functions are concise and suitable for short functions, especially callbacks.

What does this code output?
```
const square = x => x * x;
console.log(square(5));
```
   1. 10
   2. 25
   3. undefined
   4. Throws an error

Answer: 2. 25
Explanation: The arrow function implicitly returns x * x, so 5 * 5 equals 25.

What does this code output?
```
const greet = name => `Hello, ${name}!`;
console.log(greet("Alice"));
```
   1. "Hello, Alice!"
   2. undefined
   3. "Hello, !"
   4. Throws an error

Answer: 1. "Hello, Alice!"
Explanation: The arrow function takes one parameter (name) and returns the formatted string.

How do you write an arrow function with no parameters?
```
   1. const fn = => {};
   2. const fn = () => {};
   3. const fn = =>;
   4. const fn = {};
```

Answer: 2. `const fn = () => {};`
Explanation: For no parameters, parentheses are required before the =>.

What does this code output?
```
const multiply = (a, b = 2) => a * b;
console.log(multiply(5));
```
1. 5
2. 10
3. 15
4. Throws an error

Answer: 2. 10
Explanation: The arrow function uses a default parameter value for b. Since b is not provided, it defaults to 2, so 5 * 2 = 10.

What is the output of this code?
```
const divide = (a, b) => {
   if (b === 0) return "Cannot divide by
zero";
   return a / b;
};
console.log(divide(10, 0));
```
1. 0
2. "Cannot divide by zero"
3. Infinity
4. Throws an error

Answer: 2. "Cannot divide by zero"
Explanation: The arrow function checks if b === 0 and returns the error message before attempting division.

Which of the following is not true about arrow functions?

1. They are concise and easy to write.
2. They do not have their own `this`.
3. They can be used as methods in objects.
4. They cannot have default parameters.

Answer: 4. They cannot have default parameters.
Explanation: Arrow functions can have default parameters, like any other function.

What does this code output?

```
const person = {
  name: "Alice",
  greet: () => {
    console.log(`Hello, ${this.name}`);
  }
};
person.greet();
```

1. "Hello, Alice"
2. "Hello, undefined"
3. Throws an error
4. "Hello, null"

Answer: 2. "Hello, undefined"
Explanation: Arrow functions do not have their own `this`, so `this.name` refers to the `this` of the outer scope, which in this case is undefined.

What happens if you use the arguments object in an arrow function?

1. It works the same as in a regular function.
2. It refers to the arguments passed to the enclosing scope.
3. It throws an error.

4. It creates a new `arguments` object.

Answer: 2. It refers to the arguments passed to the enclosing scope.
Explanation: Arrow functions do not have their own `arguments` object and instead inherit it from their enclosing scope.

What does this code output?

```
const numbers = [1, 2, 3];
const result = numbers.filter(num => num > 1);
console.log(result);
```

1. `[1]`
2. `[2, 3]`
3. `[1, 2, 3]`
4. Throws an error

Answer: 2. `[2, 3]`
Explanation: The `filter` method uses the arrow function to include only elements greater than 1.

How do arrow functions handle the this keyword?

1. They create a new `this` binding.
2. They use the global `this`.
3. They inherit `this` from their enclosing lexical scope.
4. They throw an error when `this` is used.

Answer: 3. They inherit `this` from their enclosing lexical scope.
Explanation: Arrow functions do not have their own `this` and use `this` from the outer function or scope.

What does this code output?

```
const addFive = x => x + 5;
```

```
console.log(addFive(10));
```
1. 15
2. 20
3. 10
4. Throws an error

Answer: 1. 15
Explanation: The arrow function adds 5 to the input value, so `10 + 5 = 15`.

Can an arrow function have multiple statements in its body?
1. Yes, but they must be enclosed in curly braces.
2. No, it must have a single expression.
3. Only if the statements are separated by commas.
4. Only for synchronous code.

Answer: 1. Yes, but they must be enclosed in curly braces.
Explanation: Multiple statements in an arrow function must be enclosed in {} and require an explicit `return` if a value is returned.

What does this code output?
```
const add = (a, b) => {
  return a + b;
};
console.log(add(5, 10));
```
1. 15
2. undefined
3. Throws an error
4. 5

Answer: 1. 15
Explanation: The arrow function explicitly returns the sum of a and b, which is 15.

What is a key difference between arrow functions and regular functions?

1. Arrow functions are always asynchronous.
2. Regular functions can be used as constructors, but arrow functions cannot.
3. Arrow functions have their own `this`.
4. Regular functions cannot access default parameters.

Answer: 2. Regular functions can be used as constructors, but arrow functions cannot.

Explanation: Arrow functions do not have their own `this` or `prototype`, so they cannot be used as constructors.

What does this code output?

```
const multiply = (a, b) => {
  const result = a * b;
  return result;
};
console.log(multiply(4, 5));
```

1. 20
2. 10
3. undefined
4. Throws an error

Answer: 1. 20

Explanation: The arrow function computes 4 * 5 and explicitly returns the result.

Can an arrow function return an object literal without curly braces?

1. Yes, but the object must be wrapped in parentheses.
2. No, object literals require `return`.
3. Yes, it works the same as regular functions.
4. Only for single-property objects.

Answer: 1. Yes, but the object must be wrapped in parentheses.
Explanation: Wrapping the object in parentheses distinguishes it from a block.
Example:

```
const getObject = () => ({ key: "value" });
console.log(getObject());
```

What does this code output?

```
const person = {
  name: "Alice",
  sayName: function() {
    const arrow = () =>
console.log(this.name);
    arrow();
  }
};
person.sayName();
```

1. "Alice"
2. undefined
3. Throws an error
4. null

Answer: 1. "Alice"
Explanation: The arrow function inherits this from the sayName method, which refers to the person object.

What is the output of this code?

```
const subtract = (a, b) => a - b;
console.log(subtract(10, 7));
```

1. 3
2. 17
3. 10

4. Throws an error

Answer: 1. 3

Explanation: The arrow function subtracts b from a,
resulting in 10 - 7 = 3.

Template Literals in JavaScript

Template literals, introduced in ES6 (ECMAScript 2015),
provide an enhanced way to work with strings in
JavaScript. They use backticks (`` ` ``) instead of single or
double quotes, allowing for multi-line strings, embedded
expressions, and more readable code.

1. Syntax of Template Literals

Template literals are enclosed by backticks:

```
const message = `Hello, World!`;
```

2. Key Features of Template Literals

2.1. Multi-Line Strings

Template literals allow strings to span multiple lines without
the need for concatenation or escape characters.

```
const multiLine = `This is
a multi-line
string.`;
console.log(multiLine);
// Output:
// This is
// a multi-line
// string.
```

2.2. String Interpolation

Using the ${expression} syntax, template literals can embed variables and expressions directly into strings.

```
const name = "Alice";

const age = 25;

const message = `My name is ${name}, and I am ${age} years old.`;

console.log(message);

// Output: My name is Alice, and I am 25 years old.
```

2.3. Nesting Expressions

You can perform calculations or call functions inside the ${} placeholder.

```
const a = 5;

const b = 3;

const result = `The sum of ${a} and ${b} is ${a + b}.`;

console.log(result);

// Output: The sum of 5 and 3 is 8.
```

2.4. Tagged Templates

A function can be used with template literals to customize how the strings are processed.

```
function tag(strings, ...values) {

   return strings[0] + values.map(val => val.toUpperCase()).join('');

}

const output = tag`Hello, ${"world"}!`;

console.log(output);

// Output: Hello, WORLD!
```

2.5. Escape Characters

Template literals still support escape characters like \n, \t, and \\ when needed.

3. Advantages of Template Literals

- Easier to read and write multi-line strings.
- Simplifies dynamic string construction with string interpolation.
- Provides additional power with tagged templates.

Multiple-Choice Questions

What is a template literal?

1. A string that uses single quotes (') or double quotes (") for multi-line strings.
2. A string enclosed in backticks (`) that supports multi-line strings and embedded expressions.
3. A new type of variable in JavaScript.
4. A function that processes strings dynamically.

Answer: 2. A string enclosed in backticks (`) that supports multi-line strings and embedded expressions.
Explanation: Template literals use backticks and allow features like multi-line strings and string interpolation.

What does this code output?

```
const name = "Alice";
const message = `Hello, ${name}!`;
console.log(message);
```

1. "Hello, ${name}!"
2. "Hello, Alice!"
3. "Hello, !"
4. Throws an error

Answer: 2. `"Hello, Alice!"`
Explanation: The `${name}` placeholder is replaced with the value of the name variable.

Which of the following correctly demonstrates a multi-line string using a template literal?

```
1. const text = "Line 1
     Line 2";
```
```
2. const text = `Line 1
     Line 2`;
```
```
3. const text = "Line 1\nLine 2";
```
```
4. const text = `Line 1, Line 2`;
```

Answer: 2.

```
const text = `Line 1
Line 2`;
```

Explanation: Template literals support multi-line strings natively without using escape characters.

What does this code output?

```
const a = 5;
const b = 3;
const result = `The result of ${a} + ${b}
is ${a + b}.`;
console.log(result);
```

```
1. "The result of 5 + 3 is 8."
2. "The result of a + b is 8."
3. "The result of 5 + 3 is ${a + b}."
4. Throws an error
```

Answer: 1. `"The result of 5 + 3 is 8."`
Explanation: The `${a + b}` placeholder evaluates the expression a + b and includes its result in the string.

What are backticks ( ) used for in JavaScript?
1. Defining single-line strings only.
2. Defining multi-line strings and enabling string interpolation.
3. Declaring variables.
4. Writing comments.

Answer: 2. Defining multi-line strings and enabling string interpolation.

Explanation: Backticks are used for template literals, which allow multi-line strings and embedded expressions.

What does this code output?

```
const name = "Bob";
const age = 30;
const info = `${name} is ${age} years old.`;
console.log(info);
```

1. "Bob is 30 years old."
2. "Bob is age years old."
3. "Bob is undefined years old."
4. Throws an error

Answer: 1. "Bob is 30 years old."

Explanation: The placeholders ${name} and ${age} are replaced with their respective values.

What is the output of this code?

```
const x = 10;
const y = 20;
const equation = `${x} + ${y} = ${x + y}`;
console.log(equation);
```

1. "10 + 20 = 30"
2. "10 + 20 = ${x + y}"
3. "x + y = 30"

4. Throws an error

Answer: 1. `"10 + 20 = 30"`
Explanation: The placeholders ${x}, ${y}, and ${x + y} are evaluated and included in the string.

What happens if you include a function call inside a template literal?
1. The function call is ignored.
2. The function is executed, and its result is included in the string.
3. An error is thrown.
4. The function name is included in the string.

Answer: 2. The function is executed, and its result is included in the string.
Explanation: Template literals evaluate expressions, including function calls, and embed their results.

What does this code output?
```
function tag(strings, ...values) {
  return `${strings[0]}${values.join(",
")}${strings[1]}`;
}
const output = tag`Values: ${10} and
${20}.`;
console.log(output);
```
1. `"Values: 10 and 20."`
2. `"Values: 10, 20."`
3. `"Values: 10 and 20"`
4. `"Values: 10, 20"`

Answer: 2. `"Values: 10, 20."`
Explanation: The `tag` function customizes how the template literal is processed, joining values with a comma.

What is a tagged template?
1. A template literal used with a function to customize string processing.
2. A template literal that uses variables.
3. A string with embedded HTML.
4. A reserved keyword in JavaScript.

Answer: 1. A template literal used with a function to customize string processing.

Explanation: Tagged templates use a function to process template literals differently.

What does this code output?

```
const multiLine = `This is line 1
This is line 2`;
console.log(multiLine);
```

1. "This is line 1 This is line 2"
2. "This is line 1\nThis is line 2"

```
This is line 1
This is line 2
```

4.   Throws an error

Answer: 3.

```
This is line 1
This is line 2
```

Explanation: Template literals preserve the line breaks directly, making them ideal for multi-line strings.

What happens if you use ${} inside a template literal but provide no variable or expression?
1. Throws an error.
2. Outputs an empty string.
3. Outputs ${} as is.
4. Outputs undefined.

Answer: 3. Outputs ${} as is.
Explanation: If ${} does not contain a valid variable or expression, it is treated as regular text.

What does this code output?

```
const product = "laptop";
const price = 1200;
console.log(`The ${product} costs
$${price}.`);
```

1. "The laptop costs $1200."
2. "The product costs $price."
3. "The undefined costs $undefined."
4. Throws an error

Answer: 1. "The laptop costs $1200."
Explanation: The placeholders ${product} and ${price} are replaced with their respective values.

Can you use nested template literals?

1. Yes, by embedding backticks inside ${}.
2. No, template literals cannot be nested.
3. Only in tagged templates.
4. Yes, but only with functions.

Answer: 1. Yes, by embedding backticks inside ${}.
Explanation: Nested template literals can be used by placing backticks inside ${}.
Example:

```
const inner = `inner template`;
const outer = `Outer contains: ${`Inner
says: ${inner}`}`;
console.log(outer);
// Output: Outer contains: Inner says:
inner template
```

What does this code output?

```
const a = 10;
const b = 20;
console.log(`${a} multiplied by ${b} is ${a
* b}`);
```

1. "10 multiplied by 20 is 200"
2. "a multiplied by b is 200"
3. "10 multiplied by 20 is ${a * b}"
4. Throws an error

Answer: 1. "10 multiplied by 20 is 200"
Explanation: The placeholders are replaced with the values of a, b, and the result of a * b.

What does this code output?

```
function getString() {
    return "dynamic";
}
const str = `This is a ${getString()}
string.`;
console.log(str);
```

1. "This is a dynamic string."
2. "This is a ${getString()} string."
3. "This is a undefined string."
4. Throws an error

Answer: 1. "This is a dynamic string."
Explanation: The getString() function is called, and its return value is embedded in the template literal.

Which of the following is true about template literals?
1. They only work with string variables.
2. They allow embedded expressions, including numbers and function calls.

3. They can only include variables.
4. They are not compatible with multi-line strings.

Answer: 2. They allow embedded expressions, including numbers and function calls.

Explanation: Template literals can embed any JavaScript expression using ${}.

What does this code output?

```
const age = 30;
console.log(`You are ${age >= 18 ? "an
adult" : "a minor"}.`);
```

1. "You are an adult."
2. "You are a minor."
3. "You are undefined."
4. Throws an error

Answer: 1. "You are an adult."

Explanation: The ternary operator evaluates age >= 18 and returns "an adult", which is embedded in the string.

What does this code output?

```
const x = 5;
const y = 10;
console.log(`${x + y}`);
```

1. 5 + 10
2. 15
3. "${x + y}"
4. Throws an error

Answer: 2. 15

Explanation: The expression ${x + y} evaluates x + y and embeds the result (15) in the string.

Can you use template literals for dynamic HTML content?

1. Yes, template literals are ideal for generating dynamic HTML.
2. No, template literals only work with plain strings.
3. Only with third-party libraries.
4. Only if used with innerHTML.

Answer: 1. Yes, template literals are ideal for generating dynamic HTML.
Explanation: Template literals simplify the creation of dynamic HTML by embedding variables and expressions.

What does this code output?

```
const escaped = `This is a backtick: \``;
console.log(escaped);
```

1. "This is a backtick: `"
2. "This is a backtick: \""`
3. "This is a backtick: \"`
4. Throws an error

Answer: 1. "This is a backtick: "
Explanation: Backticks inside template literals can be escaped using a backslash (`).

Which of the following uses a tagged template?

```
1. const message = `Hello, world!`;
2. const tag = strings => strings[0];
   const result = tag`Hello, tagged
   world!`;
3. const tag = `Hello, world!`;
4. const tag = () => `Hello, world!`;
```

Answer: 2.

```
const tag = strings => strings[0];
```

```
const result = tag`Hello, tagged world!`;
```
Explanation: A tagged template uses a function (tag) to process the template literal.

What is the output of this code?
```
const a = 10;
const b = 20;
const sum = `The sum of ${a} and ${b} is
${a + b}.`;
console.log(sum);
```
1. "The sum of 10 and 20 is 30."
2. "The sum of ${a} and ${b} is ${a + b}."
3. "The sum of a and b is 30."
4. Throws an error

Answer: 1. "The sum of 10 and 20 is 30."
Explanation: Template literals evaluate the placeholders and include their values in the string.

What does this code output?
```
const info = `This is a
multi-line
string.`;
console.log(info);
```
1. "This is a multi-line string."
2. "This is a \n multi-line \n string."
3. This is a
   multi-line
   string.
4. Throws an error

Answer: 3.

```
This is a
```

```
multi-line
```
```
string.
```
Explanation: Template literals preserve line breaks.

Can template literals be used for inline CSS in JavaScript?
1. Yes, they simplify inline CSS with dynamic values.
2. No, they only work with plain text.
3. Only with CSS libraries.
4. Only in HTML files.

Answer: 1. Yes, they simplify inline CSS with dynamic values.
Explanation: Template literals can be used to construct inline CSS strings dynamically.
Example:
```
const color = "blue";
const style = `color: ${color}; font-size:
16px;`;
element.style = style;
```

Destructuring and Rest/Spread Operators in JavaScript

JavaScript introduced **destructuring** and the **rest/spread operators** in ES6 (ECMAScript 2015) to simplify working with arrays, objects, and function arguments. These features make the code cleaner, more readable, and more efficient.

1. Destructuring

Destructuring allows you to extract values from arrays or properties from objects and assign them to variables in a single statement.

1.1. Array Destructuring

You can unpack elements of an array into variables.

Example:

```
const numbers = [1, 2, 3];
const [first, second, third] = numbers;
console.log(first); // Output: 1
console.log(second); // Output: 2
console.log(third); // Output: 3
```

Skipping Elements:

```
const numbers = [1, 2, 3, 4];
const [first, , third] = numbers; // Skip
the second element
console.log(first, third); // Output: 1 3
```

1.2. Object Destructuring

Extract properties of an object into variables.

Example:

```
const person = { name: "Alice", age: 25 };
const { name, age } = person;
console.log(name); // Output: Alice
console.log(age); // Output: 25
```

Renaming Variables:

```
const person = { name: "Alice", age: 25 };
const { name: fullName, age: years } =
person;
console.log(fullName); // Output: Alice
console.log(years); // Output: 25
```

Default Values:

```
const person = { name: "Alice" };
const { name, age = 30 } = person;
```

```
console.log(age); // Output: 30 (default
value)
```

2. Rest Operator

The **rest operator (...)** collects the remaining elements of an array or properties of an object into a new variable.

2.1. In Arrays

```
const [first, ...rest] = [1, 2, 3, 4];
console.log(first); // Output: 1
console.log(rest);  // Output: [2, 3, 4]
```

2.2. In Objects

```
const { name, ...others } = { name:
"Alice", age: 25, city: "New York" };
console.log(name);    // Output: Alice
console.log(others); // Output: { age: 25,
city: "New York" }
```

3. Spread Operator

The **spread operator (...)** expands an array or object into individual elements or properties.

3.1. In Arrays

```
const arr1 = [1, 2];
const arr2 = [...arr1, 3, 4];
console.log(arr2); // Output: [1, 2, 3, 4]
```

3.2. In Objects

```
const obj1 = { name: "Alice", age: 25 };
const obj2 = { ...obj1, city: "New York" };
console.log(obj2); // Output: { name:
"Alice", age: 25, city: "New York" }
```

4. Rest Parameters in Functions

The rest operator can be used to collect all arguments passed to a function into an array.

Example:

```
function sum(...nums) {
   return nums.reduce((total, num) => total + num, 0);
}
console.log(sum(1, 2, 3)); // Output: 6
```

5. Key Points

- **Destructuring** extracts data from arrays or objects into variables.
- **Rest operator** collects the remaining items into an array or object.
- **Spread operator** expands arrays or objects into individual elements or properties.
- Rest parameters in functions simplify handling an indefinite number of arguments.

Multiple-Choice Questions

What does this code output?

```
const [a, b] = [10, 20];
console.log(a, b);
```

1. 10 20
2. [10, 20]
3. undefined undefined
4. Throws an error

Answer: 1. 10 20

Explanation: The array [10, 20] is destructured, assigning 10 to a and 20 to b.

What is the rest operator (...) used for?
1. To extract specific elements from an array.
2. To collect remaining elements into an array or object.
3. To iterate over an array.
4. To concatenate two arrays.

Answer: 2. To collect remaining elements into an array or object.

Explanation: The rest operator gathers the remaining items into a single variable.

What does this code output?
```
const person = { name: "Bob", age: 30 };
const { name, ...rest } = person;
console.log(rest);
```
1. { name: "Bob" }
2. { age: 30 }
3. undefined
4. Throws an error

Answer: 2. { age: 30 }

Explanation: The ...rest collects all properties except name into the rest object.

What does this code output?
```
const nums = [1, 2, 3];
const copy = [...nums];
console.log(copy);
```
1. [1, 2, 3]
2. [[1, 2, 3]]
3. undefined
4. Throws an error

Answer: 1. `[1, 2, 3]`
Explanation: The spread operator creates a shallow copy of the nums array.

What does this code output?
```
const [a, , b] = [10, 20, 30];
console.log(a, b);
```
1. `10 30`
2. `10 20`
3. `undefined undefined`
4. Throws an error

Answer: 1. `10 30`
Explanation: The second element (20) is skipped using a comma in the destructuring pattern.

What does this code output?
```
const obj = { x: 1, y: 2 };
const newObj = { ...obj, z: 3 };
console.log(newObj);
```
1. `{ x: 1, y: 2, z: 3 }`
2. `{ x: 1, z: 3 }`
3. `{ y: 2, z: 3 }`
4. Throws an error

Answer: 1. `{ x: 1, y: 2, z: 3 }`
Explanation: The spread operator expands the properties of `obj` into newObj, adding z.

What does this code output?
```
const [first, ...rest] = [1, 2, 3, 4];
console.log(rest);
```
1. `[2, 3, 4]`
2. `[1]`

3. `undefined`
4. Throws an error

Answer: 1. `[2, 3, 4]`
Explanation: The rest operator collects all elements except the first into the `rest` array.

What is the purpose of the spread operator?

1. To extract specific properties from an object.
2. To expand an array or object into individual elements or properties.
3. To iterate over arrays.
4. To define default parameters.

Answer: 2. To expand an array or object into individual elements or properties.
Explanation: The spread operator (...) expands arrays and objects where individual items are needed.

What does this code output?

```
function sum(a, b, ...rest) {
   return rest.reduce((total, num) => total
+ num, a + b);
}
console.log(sum(1, 2, 3, 4));
```

1. `10`
2. `6`
3. `0`
4. Throws an error

Answer: 1. `10`
Explanation: The `rest` parameter collects 3 and 4, and their sum is added to `a + b`.

What does this code output?

```
const nums = [1, 2, 3];
console.log([...nums, 4]);
```

1. `[1, 2, 3, 4]`
2. `[1, 2, 3]`
3. `undefined`
4. Throws an error

Answer: 1. `[1, 2, 3, 4]`

Explanation: The spread operator expands nums into individual elements and appends 4.

Would you like the remaining 15 questions?

What does this code output?

```
const { a, b = 10 } = { a: 5 };
console.log(a, b);
```

1. `5 10`
2. `5 undefined`
3. `undefined 10`
4. Throws an error

Answer: 1. `5 10`

Explanation: The b variable gets its default value (10) because the property b is not present in the object.

What does this code output?

```
const obj = { x: 1, y: 2 };
const { x, ...rest } = obj;
console.log(rest);
```

1. `{ x: 1 }`
2. `{ y: 2 }`
3. `{}`
4. `undefined`

Answer: 2. `{ y: 2 }`

Explanation: The rest operator collects all remaining properties except x into the `rest` object.

What does this code output?
```
const [a, ...rest] = [];
console.log(a, rest);
```
    1. undefined []
    2. undefined undefined
    3. null []
    4. Throws an error

Answer: 1. undefined []
Explanation: Since the array is empty, a is undefined, and rest is an empty array.

Which of the following correctly clones an array?
    1. const arr1 = [1, 2, 3]; const arr2 = arr1;
    2. const arr1 = [1, 2, 3]; const arr2 = [...arr1];
    3. const arr1 = [1, 2, 3]; const arr2 = arr1.slice();
    4. Both 2 and 3

Answer: 4. Both 2 and 3
Explanation: Using the spread operator (...) or slice() creates a shallow copy of the array, unlike direct assignment, which creates a reference.

What does this code output?
```
const arr1 = [1, 2];
const arr2 = [...arr1, 3, 4];
console.log(arr2);
```
    1. [1, 2, 3, 4]
    2. [[1, 2], 3, 4]
    3. [3, 4]
    4. Throws an error

Answer: 1. `[1, 2, 3, 4]`
Explanation: The spread operator expands `arr1` into individual elements, followed by 3 and 4.

What does this code output?
```
const obj1 = { name: "Alice" };
const obj2 = { ...obj1, age: 25 };
console.log(obj2);
```
1. `{ name: "Alice", age: 25 }`
2. `{ age: 25 }`
3. `{ name: "Alice" }`
4. Throws an error

Answer: 1. `{ name: "Alice", age: 25 }`
Explanation: The spread operator expands the properties of `obj1` into `obj2`, then adds the age property.

What does this code output?
```
function multiply(a, b, ...rest) {
  return rest.length;
}
console.log(multiply(1, 2, 3, 4, 5));
```
1. 3
2. 5
3. 0
4. Throws an error

Answer: 1. 3
Explanation: The rest parameter collects 3, 4, and 5 into an array, so `rest.length` is 3.

What does this code output?
```
const nums = [1, 2, 3, 4];
const [a, b, ...rest] = nums;
```

```
console.log(rest);
```
1. [3, 4]
2. [1, 2]
3. [4]
4. Throws an error

Answer: 1. [3, 4]
Explanation: The rest operator collects all elements of the array after a and b into the rest array.

What does this code output?
```
const { x, y = 10 } = { x: 5 };
console.log(x, y);
```
1. 5 10
2. 5 undefined
3. undefined 10
4. Throws an error

Answer: 1. 5 10
Explanation: The y variable gets its default value of 10 because it is not present in the object.

What does this code output?
```
const obj1 = { a: 1, b: 2 };
const obj2 = { ...obj1, b: 3 };
console.log(obj2);
```
1. { a: 1, b: 2 }
2. { a: 1, b: 3 }
3. { b: 3 }
4. Throws an error

Answer: 2. { a: 1, b: 3 }
Explanation: The spread operator expands obj1 into obj2, and the b property is overwritten by the new value 3.

What does this code output?

```
const obj = { a: 1, b: 2 };
const { ...rest } = obj;
console.log(rest);
```

   1. { a: 1, b: 2 }

   2. {}

   3. undefined

   4. Throws an error

Answer: 1. { a: 1, b: 2 }

Explanation: The rest operator collects all properties of the object into the rest variable.

What does this code output?

```
const nums = [1, 2];
const total = [...nums, 3, 4].reduce((acc,
num) => acc + num, 0);
console.log(total);
```

   1. 10

   2. [1, 2, 3, 4]

   3. undefined

   4. Throws an error

Answer: 1. 10

Explanation: The spread operator expands nums into a new array [1, 2, 3, 4], and reduce computes their sum.

What does this code output?

```
function joinStrings(...strings) {
   return strings.join(", ");
}
console.log(joinStrings("Alice", "Bob",
"Charlie"));
```

1. "Alice, Bob, Charlie"
2. "Alice Bob Charlie"
3. ["Alice", "Bob", "Charlie"]
4. Throws an error

Answer: 1. "Alice, Bob, Charlie"
Explanation: The rest parameter collects all arguments into an array, and `join` concatenates them with commas.

What does this code output?
```
const arr1 = [1, 2];
const arr2 = [...arr1, ...[3, 4]];
console.log(arr2);
```
1. [1, 2, 3, 4]
2. [1, 2, [3, 4]]
3. undefined
4. Throws an error

Answer: 1. [1, 2, 3, 4]
Explanation: The spread operator expands both arrays into individual elements, creating a new array.

What does this code output?
```
const obj1 = { a: 1, b: 2 };
const obj2 = { b: 3, c: 4 };
const merged = { ...obj1, ...obj2 };
console.log(merged);
```
1. { a: 1, b: 3, c: 4 }
2. { a: 1, b: 2, c: 4 }
3. { b: 3, c: 4 }
4. Throws an error

Answer: 1. { a: 1, b: 3, c: 4 }
Explanation: The spread operator merges the properties

of obj1 and obj2. Since both have b, the value from obj2 overwrites the one in obj1.

Let me know if you'd like further explanations or assistance!

Promises and .then() Chaining in JavaScript

Promises in JavaScript are used to handle asynchronous operations like fetching data, reading files, or waiting for timers. They provide a cleaner and more manageable way to work with asynchronous code compared to callbacks, reducing "callback hell."

1. What is a Promise?

A **Promise** is an object representing the eventual completion (or failure) of an asynchronous operation. It can be in one of three states:

- **Pending**: The initial state, neither fulfilled nor rejected.
- **Fulfilled**: The operation completed successfully.
- **Rejected**: The operation failed.

2. Creating a Promise

A Promise is created using the `Promise` constructor, which takes a function (executor) with two parameters: `resolve` and `reject`.

Example:

```
const myPromise = new Promise((resolve,
reject) => {
  const success = true;
  if (success) {
    resolve("Operation successful!");
  } else {
```

```
    reject("Operation failed.");
  }
});
```

3. Handling Promises with .then() and .catch()

- **.then()**: Used to handle the fulfillment of a Promise.
- **.catch()**: Used to handle the rejection of a Promise.

Example:

```
myPromise
  .then((result) => {
    console.log(result); // Logs "Operation
successful!" if resolved
  })
  .catch((error) => {
    console.error(error); // Logs
"Operation failed." if rejected
  });
```

4. Chaining Promises with .then()

Promises can be chained together, where each .then() returns a new Promise.

Example:

```
const promiseChain = new Promise((resolve)
=> {
  resolve(10);
});
promiseChain
  .then((value) => {
    console.log(value); // Logs 10
```

```
    return value * 2;
})
.then((value) => {
  console.log(value); // Logs 20
  return value + 5;
})
.then((value) => {
  console.log(value); // Logs 25
});
```

5. Error Handling in Chained Promises

Errors in any .then() block are passed down to the next .catch() block.

Example:

```
const errorChain = new Promise((resolve,
reject) => {
  reject("An error occurred.");
});
errorChain
  .then((value) => {
    console.log(value); // This is skipped
  })
  .catch((error) => {
    console.error(error); // Logs "An error
occurred."
    return "Recovered";
  })
  .then((value) => {
    console.log(value); // Logs "Recovered"
  });
```

6. Returning Promises from .then()

A `.then()` block can return another Promise, creating a nested chain.

Example:

```
const delayedPromise = (value) =>
  new Promise((resolve) => {
    setTimeout(() => resolve(value), 1000);
  });
delayedPromise(5)
  .then((value) => {
    console.log(value); // Logs 5 after 1
second
    return delayedPromise(value * 2);
  })
  .then((value) => {
    console.log(value); // Logs 10 after
another second
  });
```

7. Key Points

- Promises simplify asynchronous operations by avoiding deeply nested callbacks.
- `.then()` and `.catch()` handle the resolved or rejected state of a Promise.
- `.then()` can return a value, another Promise, or nothing (implicitly returning `undefined`).
- Errors propagate down the chain and can be caught using `.catch()`.

Multiple-Choice Questions

What is the initial state of a Promise?
1. Fulfilled
2. Rejected
3. Pending
4. Completed

Answer: 3. Pending
Explanation: Promises start in the pending state, indicating that the operation is not yet completed.

What does the resolve function do in a Promise?
1. Marks the Promise as fulfilled and provides a result.
2. Marks the Promise as rejected.
3. Cancels the Promise.
4. Executes the .catch() block.

Answer: 1. Marks the Promise as fulfilled and provides a result.
Explanation: Calling resolve changes the Promise state to fulfilled and passes the result to the .then() handlers.

What does this code output?
```
const promise = new Promise((resolve) => {
  resolve("Success!");
});
promise.then((result) => {
  console.log(result);
});
```
1. "Success!"
2. undefined
3. Throws an error
4. null

Answer: 1. "Success!"
Explanation: The Promise is resolved with "Success!", which is passed to the .then() handler.

What does the .catch() method do?
1. Handles fulfilled Promises.
2. Handles rejected Promises.
3. Cancels a Promise.
4. Resolves a Promise.

Answer: 2. Handles rejected Promises.
Explanation: The .catch() method is used to handle errors or rejections in a Promise chain.

What does this code output?

```
const promise = Promise.reject("Error!");
promise.catch((error) => {
  console.log(error);
});
```

1. "Error!"
2. undefined
3. Throws an error
4. null

Answer: 1. "Error!"
Explanation: The Promise is rejected with "Error!", which is passed to the .catch() handler.

What does this code output?

```
const promise = new Promise((resolve) => {
  resolve(5);
});
promise
   .then((value) => value * 2)
   .then((value) => console.log(value));
```

1. 5
2. 10
3. `undefined`
4. Throws an error

Answer: 2. 10
Explanation: Each `.then()` handler processes the value from the previous one. The first `.then()` doubles 5 to 10, which is logged by the second.

What is the purpose of returning a Promise in a .then() block?
1. To cancel the chain.
2. To create a nested chain that waits for the new Promise to resolve.
3. To skip the next `.then()` block.
4. To end the chain.

Answer: 2. To create a nested chain that waits for the new Promise to resolve.
Explanation: Returning a Promise allows chaining and ensures that the next `.then()` waits for it to resolve.

What does this code output?

```
const promise = new Promise((resolve) => {
  resolve(3);
});
promise
  .then((value) => {
    console.log(value);
    return value + 2;
  })
  .then((value) => {
    console.log(value);
  });
```

1. 3, 5
2. 5, 3
3. 3, undefined
4. Throws an error

Answer: 1. 3, 5
Explanation: The first `.then()` logs 3 and returns 5. The second `.then()` logs the returned value 5.

What does this code output?

```
Promise.resolve(10)
    .then((value) => value + 5)
    .catch((error) => console.error(error))
    .then((value) => console.log(value));
```

1. 10
2. 15
3. undefined
4. Throws an error

Answer: 2. 15
Explanation: The `.then()` adds 5 to 10, and the second `.then()` logs the result since there's no error.

What happens if an error is thrown inside a .then() block?

1. The Promise is fulfilled.
2. The chain is broken.
3. The error is passed to the next `.catch()` block.
4. The chain stops immediately.

Answer: 3. The error is passed to the next `.catch()` block.
Explanation: Errors inside `.then()` are caught by the next `.catch()` in the chain.

What does this code output?

```
const promise = new Promise((resolve,
reject) => {
  reject("Failure");
});
promise
  .then((value) => {
    console.log(value);
    return value;
  })
  .catch((error) => {
    console.error(error);
    return "Recovered";
  })
  .then((value) => {
    console.log(value);
  });
```

1. "Failure", "Recovered"
2. Throws an error
3. "Failure"
4. "Recovered"

Answer: 1. "Failure", "Recovered"
Explanation: The reject triggers the .catch() block, which logs "Failure" and returns "Recovered". The subsequent .then() logs "Recovered".

What does this code output?

```
const promise = Promise.resolve(20);
promise
  .then((value) => {
    throw new Error("An error occurred");
```

```
})
.catch((error) => {
  console.error(error.message);
  return 25;
})
.then((value) => {
  console.log(value);
});
```
1. "An error occurred", 25
2. "An error occurred"
3. Throws an error
4. 20, 25

Answer: 1. "An error occurred", 25
Explanation: The .then() throws an error, triggering the .catch() block, which logs the error message and returns 25. The final .then() logs 25.

What does this code output?
```
Promise.resolve(5)
  .then((value) => value * 2)
  .then((value) => Promise.resolve(value +
10))
  .then((value) => console.log(value));
```
1. 5
2. 20
3. 15
4. Throws an error

Answer: 2. 20
Explanation: The first .then() doubles 5 to 10, the second .then() adds 10 to return a resolved Promise of 20, and the final .then() logs 20.

Which statement is true about chaining Promises?

1. Each `.then()` block waits for the previous one to resolve.
2. Each `.then()` block executes simultaneously.
3. Promises in a chain share the same state.
4. Errors in one block do not affect subsequent blocks.

Answer: 1. Each `.then()` block waits for the previous one to resolve.

Explanation: `.then()` chaining ensures sequential execution, where each `.then()` waits for the previous one to complete.

What does this code output?

```
const promise = new Promise((resolve) => {
  setTimeout(() => resolve(42), 1000);
});
promise
  .then((value) => value + 1)
  .then((value) => console.log(value));
```

1. 42
2. 43
3. Throws an error
4. Logs nothing

Answer: 2. 43

Explanation: The Promise resolves to 42 after 1 second. The first `.then()` adds 1 to return 43, which is logged by the second `.then()`.

What does this code output?

```
Promise.reject("Error!")
  .catch((error) => {
    console.error(error);
    return "Recovered";
```

```
})
.then((value) => {
  console.log(value);
});
```

1. "Error!", "Recovered"
2. "Recovered"
3. "Error!"
4. Throws an error

Answer: 1. "Error!", "Recovered"
Explanation: The .catch() logs "Error!" and returns
"Recovered". The .then() logs the returned value
"Recovered".

What does this code output?

```
Promise.resolve(10)
  .then((value) => {
    if (value > 5) throw "Value too high";
    return value;
  })
  .catch((error) => {
    console.error(error);
    return 0;
  })
  .then((value) => {
    console.log(value);
  });
```

1. "Value too high", 0
2. 10
3. 0
4. Throws an error

Answer: 1. `"Value too high", 0`
Explanation: The first `.then()` throws an error, which is caught by `.catch()` that logs the error and returns 0. The final `.then()` logs 0.

What happens when you return undefined in a .then() block?
1. The chain stops.
2. The next `.then()` receives `undefined`.
3. The next `.then()` block is skipped.
4. The Promise is rejected.

Answer: 2. The next `.then()` receives `undefined`.
Explanation: Returning `undefined` explicitly or implicitly passes `undefined` to the next `.then()` block.

What does this code output?
```
Promise.resolve(5)
  .then((value) => {
    console.log(value);
    return Promise.reject("Error
occurred");
  })
  .catch((error) => {
    console.error(error);
  });
```
1. `5, "Error occurred"`
2. `"Error occurred"`
3. `5`
4. Throws an error

Answer: 1. `5, "Error occurred"`
Explanation: The first `.then()` logs 5 and returns a

rejected Promise, triggering the `.catch()` block to log
"`Error occurred`".

What is the purpose of returning a value in .then()?
1. To create a new Promise.
2. To pass the value to the next `.then()`.
3. To reject the chain.
4. To skip the next `.then()` block.

Answer: 2. To pass the value to the next `.then()`.
Explanation: Returning a value from `.then()` sends it to the next `.then()` in the chain.

What does this code output?
```
const promise = new Promise((resolve) => {
  resolve(10);
});
promise
  .then((value) => value + 5)
  .then((value) => Promise.resolve(value *
2))
  .then((value) => console.log(value));
```
1. 20
2. 30
3. 15
4. Throws an error

Answer: 2. 30
Explanation: The first `.then()` adds 5 to return 15, the second `.then()` doubles it to return 30, and the final `.then()` logs 30.

What does this code output?
```
Promise.resolve(5)
```

```
.then((value) => {
  console.log(value);
  return value * 2;
})
.catch((error) => {
  console.error(error);
})
.then((value) => {
  console.log(value);
});
```
1. 5, 10
2. 5, undefined
3. 5
4. Throws an error

Answer: 1. 5, 10
Explanation: The first .then() logs 5 and returns 10.
The .catch() is skipped because there's no error, so the
final .then() logs 10.

What does this code output?
```
Promise.reject("Initial error")
  .catch((error) => {
    console.error(error);
    throw "New error";
  })
  .catch((error) => {
    console.error(error);
  });
```
1. "Initial error", "New error"
2. "Initial error"
3. "New error"

4. Throws an error

Answer: 1. `"Initial error"`, `"New error"`
Explanation: The first `.catch()` logs `"Initial error"` and throws `"New error"`. The second `.catch()` logs `"New error"`.

What does this code output?
```
const promise = new Promise((resolve,
reject) => {
  reject("Error");
});
promise
  .catch((error) => {
    console.error(error);
    return 42;
  })
  .then((value) => {
    console.log(value);
  });
```
1. `"Error"`, 42
2. `"Error"`
3. 42
4. Throws an error

Answer: 1. `"Error"`, 42
Explanation: The `.catch()` logs `"Error"` and returns 42. The `.then()` logs 42.

What does this code output?
```
Promise.resolve(100)
  .then((value) => {
    console.log(value);
    return value + 50;
```

```
})
.then((value) => {
  console.log(value);
  throw "Unexpected error";
})
.catch((error) => {
  console.error(error);
});
```

1. 100, 150, "Unexpected error"
2. 100, 150
3. "Unexpected error"
4. Throws an error

Answer: 1. 100, 150, "Unexpected error"
Explanation: The first .then() logs 100 and returns 150, the second .then() logs 150 and throws an error, and the .catch() logs "Unexpected error".

Browser Storage in JavaScript (localStorage and sessionStorage)

Browser storage in JavaScript allows developers to store data directly in a user's browser. The two primary storage mechanisms are **localStorage** and **sessionStorage**, both part of the Web Storage API.

1. What is Browser Storage?

Browser storage provides a way to save key-value pairs locally in the user's browser. This data persists either for the duration of the session or indefinitely, depending on the storage type.

2. localStorage

- **Purpose**: Stores data with no expiration time.
- **Persistence**: Data remains available even after the browser is closed and reopened.
- **Capacity**: Approximately 5MB per origin (may vary by browser).

Examples:

Set Data:

```
localStorage.setItem("username", "Alice");
```

Get Data:

```
const username =
localStorage.getItem("username");

console.log(username); // Output: Alice
```

Remove Data:

```
localStorage.removeItem("username");
```

Clear All Data:

```
localStorage.clear();
```

3. sessionStorage

- **Purpose**: Stores data for the duration of the browser session.
- **Persistence**: Data is cleared when the tab or browser is closed.
- **Capacity**: Approximately 5MB per origin (same as localStorage).

Examples:

Set Data:

```
sessionStorage.setItem("sessionId",
"12345");
```

Get Data:

```
const sessionId =
sessionStorage.getItem("sessionId");

console.log(sessionId); // Output: 12345
```

Remove Data:

```
sessionStorage.removeItem("sessionId");
```
Clear All Data:

```
sessionStorage.clear();
```

4. Key Differences Between localStorage and sessionStorage

Feature	localStorage	sessionStorage
Persistence	Data persists indefinitely.	Data persists only for the session.
Scope	Shared across all tabs for the same origin.	Unique to each tab or window.
Capacity	~5MB per origin.	~5MB per origin.

5. Storage API Methods

Both `localStorage` and `sessionStorage` share the same API:

Method	Description
`setItem(key, value)`	Stores a key-value pair.
`getItem(key)`	Retrieves the value for the given key.
`removeItem(key)`	Removes the key-value pair for the given key.

`clear()`	Clears all key-value pairs in the storage.
`length`	Returns the number of stored key-value pairs.
`key(index)`	Retrieves the key at the given index.

6. Data Types in Storage

Browser storage can only store strings. If you want to store objects or arrays, you need to convert them to strings using `JSON.stringify()` and back to their original form with `JSON.parse()`.

Example:

```
const user = { name: "Alice", age: 25 };
// Save object as string
localStorage.setItem("user",
JSON.stringify(user));
// Retrieve and parse back to object
const retrievedUser =
JSON.parse(localStorage.getItem("user"));
console.log(retrievedUser.name); // Output:
Alice
```

7. Security Considerations

- Avoid storing sensitive data like passwords or credit card details in browser storage.
- Browser storage is accessible via JavaScript, making it vulnerable to XSS attacks.

Multiple-Choice Questions

What is the key difference between localStorage and sessionStorage?

1. `localStorage` data is cleared when the tab is closed; `sessionStorage` persists indefinitely.
2. `localStorage` persists indefinitely; `sessionStorage` is cleared when the tab is closed.
3. `localStorage` can only store strings; `sessionStorage` can store objects.
4. `localStorage` is accessible across tabs, while `sessionStorage` is not.

Answer: 2. `localStorage` persists indefinitely; `sessionStorage` is cleared when the tab is closed.
Explanation: `localStorage` retains data even after the browser is closed, while `sessionStorage` only lasts for the session.

What does localStorage.setItem("key", "value") do?

1. Adds a new key-value pair to `localStorage`.
2. Replaces all existing key-value pairs in `localStorage`.
3. Clears `localStorage`.
4. Retrieves a value from `localStorage`.

Answer: 1. Adds a new key-value pair to `localStorage`.
Explanation: The `setItem` method stores a new key-value pair in `localStorage`.

What will this code output?

```
localStorage.setItem("user", "Alice");
console.log(localStorage.getItem("user"));
```

1. `Alice`

2. `null`
3. `undefined`
4. Throws an error

Answer: 1. `Alice`
Explanation: The `getItem` method retrieves the value for the key `"user"` from `localStorage`.

What happens when you call localStorage.clear()?
1. Clears the current tab's storage.
2. Deletes all key-value pairs from `localStorage`.
3. Deletes all data from both `localStorage` and `sessionStorage`.
4. Throws an error.

Answer: 2. Deletes all key-value pairs from `localStorage`.
Explanation: The `clear` method removes all entries from `localStorage`.

What does localStorage.length return?
1. The total size of the stored data in bytes.
2. The number of key-value pairs stored.
3. The number of keys currently accessed.
4. Throws an error.

Answer: 2. The number of key-value pairs stored.
Explanation: The `length` property gives the total number of entries in `localStorage`.

What does this code output?
```
sessionStorage.setItem("color", "blue");
console.log(sessionStorage.getItem("color")
);
```
1. `blue`
2. `null`

3. `undefined`
4. Throws an error

Answer: 1. `blue`
Explanation: The `getItem` method retrieves the value `"blue"` for the key `"color"` from `sessionStorage`.

What happens if you attempt to retrieve a non-existent key from localStorage?
1. It throws an error.
2. It returns `undefined`.
3. It returns `null`.
4. It creates the key with an empty value.

Answer: 3. It returns `null`.
Explanation: If the key does not exist in `localStorage`, `getItem` returns `null`.

What does this code output?
```
const key = localStorage.key(0);
console.log(key);
```
1. The key at index 0 in `localStorage`.
2. The first value in `localStorage`.
3. `null`
4. Throws an error.

Answer: 1. The key at index 0 in `localStorage`.
Explanation: The key method retrieves the key at the specified index in `localStorage`.

Which method would you use to remove a specific key-value pair from localStorage?
1. `localStorage.deleteItem()`
2. `localStorage.clear()`
3. `localStorage.removeItem()`
4. `localStorage.remove()`

Answer: 3. `localStorage.removeItem()`
Explanation: The `removeItem` method deletes a specific key-value pair from `localStorage`.

Can localStorage and sessionStorage store objects directly?
1. Yes, they can store objects natively.
2. No, only strings can be stored, and objects must be stringified.
3. Yes, but only with a plugin.
4. No, only primitive values can be stored.

Answer: 2. No, only strings can be stored, and objects must be stringified.
Explanation: Both `localStorage` and `sessionStorage` only store strings. Use `JSON.stringify()` and `JSON.parse()` for objects.

What does this code output?
```
localStorage.setItem("count", 10);
console.log(typeof
localStorage.getItem("count"));
```
1. `"number"`
2. `"string"`
3. `"undefined"`
4. Throws an error

Answer: 2. `"string"`
Explanation: All values in `localStorage` and `sessionStorage` are stored as strings, even if the input is a number.

What does this code output after the browser is closed and reopened?
```
localStorage.setItem("theme", "dark");
console.log(localStorage.getItem("theme"));
```

1. `"dark"`
2. `null`
3. `undefined`
4. Throws an error

Answer: 1. `"dark"`

Explanation: Data stored in `localStorage` persists even after the browser is closed and reopened.

What happens to data stored in sessionStorage when the tab is closed?
1. It is cleared automatically.
2. It persists across browser tabs.
3. It throws an error when accessed.
4. It remains until the browser is completely closed.

Answer: 1. It is cleared automatically.

Explanation: `sessionStorage` data is specific to a browser tab and is cleared when the tab is closed.

What does this code output?

```
sessionStorage.setItem("user",
JSON.stringify({ name: "Alice" }));
const user =
JSON.parse(sessionStorage.getItem("user"));
console.log(user.name);
```

1. `"Alice"`
2. `null`
3. `undefined`
4. Throws an error

Answer: 1. `"Alice"`

Explanation: The object is stringified before storing in `sessionStorage`, and `JSON.parse()` converts it back to an object when retrieved.

Which of the following is a valid use of the localStorage API?1.

1. `localStorage.store("key", "value");`
2. `localStorage.addItem("key", "value");`
3. `localStorage.setItem("key", "value");`
4. `localStorage.pushItem("key", "value");`

Answer: 3.

`localStorage.setItem("key", "value");`

Explanation: The `setItem` method is used to store key-value pairs in `localStorage`.

What does sessionStorage.length return?

1. The size of stored data in bytes.
2. The number of keys stored in `sessionStorage`.
3. The size of `sessionStorage` capacity remaining.
4. Throws an error.

Answer: 2. The number of keys stored in `sessionStorage`.

Explanation: The `length` property of `sessionStorage` returns the number of key-value pairs stored.

What happens when you store a duplicate key in localStorage?

1. The old value is replaced by the new value.
2. Both values are stored under the same key.
3. The new value is ignored.
4. Throws an error.

Answer: 1. The old value is replaced by the new value.
Explanation: Storing a duplicate key in `localStorage` overwrites the existing value with the new one.

What does this code output?

`localStorage.setItem("key1", "value1");`

```
localStorage.setItem("key2", "value2");
console.log(localStorage.key(1));
```
1. "key1"
2. "key2"
3. null
4. Depends on the browser's key ordering.

Answer: 4. Depends on the browser's key ordering.
Explanation: The order of keys in `localStorage` is not guaranteed and may vary by browser implementation.

What is the maximum size of data that can typically be stored in localStorage or sessionStorage?
1. 2MB
2. 5MB
3. 10MB
4. Unlimited

Answer: 2. 5MB
Explanation: Most modern browsers allow approximately 5MB of data storage per origin in both `localStorage` and `sessionStorage`.

Which of the following methods clears all data from sessionStorage?
1. `sessionStorage.removeItem("key")`
2. `sessionStorage.deleteAll()`
3. `sessionStorage.clear()`
4. `sessionStorage.flush()`

Answer: 3. `sessionStorage.clear()`
Explanation: The `clear` method removes all key-value pairs from `sessionStorage`.

What does this code output if the key does not exist?
```
console.log(sessionStorage.getItem("nonexis
tentKey"));
```

1. undefined
2. null
3. Throws an error
4. " "

Answer: 2. null
Explanation: If a key does not exist in sessionStorage, getItem returns null.

Can data stored in localStorage be accessed by other domains?
1. Yes, if the domains share the same IP.
2. No, it is restricted to the same origin.
3. Yes, but only in incognito mode.
4. No, unless explicitly shared using JavaScript.

Answer: 2. No, it is restricted to the same origin.
Explanation: Data in localStorage is tied to the origin (protocol, domain, and port) and cannot be accessed by other domains.

What does this code output?
```
localStorage.setItem("value",
JSON.stringify([1, 2, 3]));
const array =
JSON.parse(localStorage.getItem("value"));
console.log(array[1]);
```
1. 1
2. 2
3. [1, 2, 3]
4. Throws an error

Answer: 2. 2
Explanation: The array is stored as a string in localStorage using JSON.stringify(). Retrieving and parsing it allows access to its elements.

What happens if localStorage is full?

1. The browser automatically clears the oldest data.
2. An error is thrown when trying to add new data.
3. New data overwrites the oldest data.
4. Nothing happens; the new data is ignored.

Answer: 2. An error is thrown when trying to add new data.
Explanation: When `localStorage` exceeds its capacity, attempting to store additional data results in a `QuotaExceededError`.

Which of the following is not a valid use case for localStorage?

1. Storing user preferences.
2. Caching data for offline use.
3. Storing sensitive data like passwords.
4. Saving a user's last visited page.

Answer: 3. Storing sensitive data like passwords.
Explanation: Storing sensitive data like passwords in `localStorage` is not secure, as it is vulnerable to JavaScript-based attacks like XSS.

Working with Cookies in JavaScript

Cookies are small pieces of data stored on the client side (browser) that websites use to store information such as user preferences, session data, and tracking information. JavaScript provides a way to create, read, and delete cookies.

1. What Are Cookies?

- Cookies are small text files stored by the browser.
- They are sent with every HTTP request to the server.
- Commonly used for:

- o User authentication
- o Session tracking
- o Storing user preferences

2. Basic Operations with Cookies

Cookies can be manipulated using the `document.cookie` property. However, `document.cookie` behaves as a single string, where all cookies for a domain are concatenated.

Setting a Cookie

Syntax:

```
document.cookie = "key=value";
```

Example:

```
document.cookie = "username=Alice";
```

Reading Cookies

Syntax:

```
const cookies = document.cookie;
```

Example:

```
console.log(document.cookie); // Output:
"username=Alice"
```

Updating a Cookie

To update a cookie, set it again with the same name but a different value.

Example:

```
document.cookie = "username=Bob";
```

Deleting a Cookie

To delete a cookie, set its `expires` attribute to a past date.

Example:

```
document.cookie = "username=; expires=Thu,
01 Jan 1970 00:00:00 UTC;";
```

3. Attributes of Cookies

Cookies can include additional attributes:

Attribute	Description
`expires`	Sets the expiration date of the cookie. Defaults to the end of the browser session if not set.
`max-age`	Specifies the lifetime of the cookie in seconds.
`path`	Specifies the URL path that must exist for the cookie to be sent.
`domain`	Specifies the domain for which the cookie is valid.
`secure`	Ensures the cookie is sent only over HTTPS connections.
`HttpOnly`	Prevents the cookie from being accessed via JavaScript, enhancing security.
`SameSite`	Restricts cookies to first-party contexts (`Strict`) or allows third-party use (`Lax` or `None`).

4. Examples

Setting a Cookie with Attributes

```
document.cookie = "user=John; max-age=3600;
path=/; secure";
```

- `user=John`: Sets the cookie's key-value pair.
- `max-age=3600`: The cookie expires in 1 hour (3600 seconds).

- `path=/`: The cookie is accessible across the entire website.
- `secure`: Ensures the cookie is sent only over HTTPS.

Reading All Cookies

```
console.log(document.cookie);
// Output: "user=John; theme=dark"
```

Deleting a Specific Cookie

```
document.cookie = "user=; expires=Thu, 01
Jan 1970 00:00:00 UTC; path=/;";
```

5. Limitations of Cookies

- **Size Limit**: Each cookie is limited to ~4KB.
- **Number of Cookies**: Browsers typically limit the number of cookies per domain (~50-100).
- **Security**: Cookies are susceptible to cross-site scripting (XSS) attacks if not secured.

6. Use Cases for Cookies

1. **Session Management**: Tracking logged-in users.
2. **Personalization**: Storing user preferences (e.g., theme).
3. **Analytics and Tracking**: Tracking user behavior across websites.

Multiple-Choice Questions

What does document.cookie return?

1. An array of all cookies.
2. A single string containing all cookies for the current domain.
3. An object with cookie key-value pairs.

4. Undefined if no cookies are set.

Answer: 2. A single string containing all cookies for the current domain.

Explanation: `document.cookie` returns all cookies as a semicolon-separated string.

Which attribute ensures a cookie is sent only over HTTPS?

1. `path`
2. `HttpOnly`
3. `secure`
4. `SameSite`

Answer: 3. `secure`

Explanation: The `secure` attribute ensures that cookies are transmitted only over HTTPS connections.

What does this code output?

```
document.cookie = "username=Alice";
console.log(document.cookie);
```

1. `"username=Alice"`
2. `"Alice"`
3. `null`
4. Throws an error

Answer: 1. `"username=Alice"`

Explanation: The `document.cookie` property sets and retrieves the current cookies.

What happens if you set a cookie without specifying an expiration date?

1. The cookie lasts until the browser is closed.
2. The cookie lasts for 24 hours.
3. The cookie is stored indefinitely.
4. The cookie is not saved.

Answer: 1. The cookie lasts until the browser is closed.
Explanation: Cookies without an expiration date are session cookies and are cleared when the browser is closed.

What does this code do?
```
document.cookie = "user=John; max-age=3600";
```
1. Deletes the cookie named user after 3600 seconds.
2. Sets a cookie named user that expires in 1 hour.
3. Sets a cookie named user that is cleared when the browser is closed.
4. Sets a secure cookie.

Answer: 2. Sets a cookie named user that expires in 1 hour.
Explanation: The max-age attribute specifies the cookie's lifespan in seconds.

What does this code output if no cookies are set?
```
console.log(document.cookie);
```
1. " " (an empty string)
2. null
3. undefined
4. Throws an error

Answer: 1. " " (an empty string)
Explanation: If no cookies are set, document.cookie returns an empty string.

How do you delete a cookie named user?.
1. document.cookie = "user=; expires=Thu, 01 Jan 1970 00:00:00 UTC;";
2. document.cookie = "user=null;";
3. document.cookie = "user=; max-age=0;";

4. Both 1 and 3

Answer: 4. Both 1 and 3

Explanation: Setting `expires` to a past date or `max-age` to 0 deletes the cookie.

Which of the following attributes prevents JavaScript from accessing cookies?
1. `secure`
2. `HttpOnly`
3. `SameSite`
4. `max-age`

Answer: 2. `HttpOnly`

Explanation: The `HttpOnly` attribute ensures cookies are not accessible via JavaScript, enhancing security.

What is the maximum size of a single cookie?
1. 1KB
2. 2KB
3. 4KB
4. 8KB

Answer: 3. 4KB

Explanation: Most browsers limit individual cookies to approximately 4KB in size.

What does the SameSite attribute do?
1. Limits cookies to secure connections only.
2. Restricts cookies to first-party or same-site contexts.
3. Prevents cookies from being accessed via JavaScript.
4. Sets the expiration date for a cookie.

Answer: 2. Restricts cookies to first-party or same-site contexts.

Explanation: The `SameSite` attribute prevents cookies

from being sent with cross-site requests unless explicitly allowed.

Which of the following is the correct syntax to set a cookie that is accessible only for a specific path?.

1. `document.cookie = "username=Alice; path=/dashboard";`
2. `document.cookie = "username=Alice; directory=/dashboard";`
3. `document.cookie = "username=Alice; folder=/dashboard";`
4. `document.cookie = "username=Alice; route=/dashboard";`

Answer: 1.

```
document.cookie = "username=Alice;
path=/dashboard";
```

Explanation: The `path` attribute specifies the URL path for which the cookie is valid.

What does this code output?

```
document.cookie = "theme=dark";
document.cookie = "font=large";
console.log(document.cookie);
```

1. `"theme=dark; font=large"`
2. `"theme=dark"`
3. `"font=large"`
4. Throws an error

Answer: 1. `"theme=dark; font=large"`

Explanation: `document.cookie` contains all cookies for the current domain and path, concatenated as a single string.

Which attribute ensures that cookies are sent only in same-site requests and not with cross-site requests?

1. `secure`
2. `path`
3. `SameSite`
4. `HttpOnly`

Answer: 3. `SameSite`

Explanation: The `SameSite` attribute prevents cookies from being sent with cross-site requests unless explicitly configured.

What happens if multiple cookies have the same name but different paths?

1. The most recently set cookie is used.
2. The cookie with the longest path is used.
3. Cookies are stored separately based on their paths.
4. Throws an error.

Answer: 3. Cookies are stored separately based on their paths.

Explanation: Cookies with the same name can coexist if their `path` attributes differ.

Which method should you use to store JSON data in a cookie?

1. Use `JSON.stringify()` before storing the data.
2. Use `JSON.parse()` before storing the data.
3. Use `setJSON()` instead of `setItem()`.
4. Cookies cannot store JSON data.

Answer: 1. Use `JSON.stringify()` before storing the data.

Explanation: Cookies can only store strings, so JSON data must be converted to a string using `JSON.stringify()`.

What does this code output?

```
document.cookie = "test=123; max-age=3600";
console.log(document.cookie.includes("test=
123"));
```

1. true
2. false
3. undefined
4. Throws an error

Answer: 1. true
Explanation: The cookie test=123 is set with a max-age of 3600 seconds and is available via document.cookie.

Which of the following is not a valid cookie attribute?

1. secure
2. path
3. HttpOnly
4. visible

Answer: 4. visible
Explanation: visible is not a valid cookie attribute. Valid attributes include secure, path, HttpOnly, and others.

What is the default behavior if the path attribute is not specified when setting a cookie?

1. The cookie is valid for the entire domain.
2. The cookie is valid for the current directory and its subdirectories.
3. The cookie is invalid.
4. Throws an error.

Answer: 2. The cookie is valid for the current directory and its subdirectories.
Explanation: If the path attribute is not specified, the cookie is restricted to the directory of the page that set it and its subdirectories.

What happens if the secure attribute is set but the site is accessed over HTTP?

1. The cookie is still sent but triggers a warning.
2. The cookie is ignored and not sent.
3. The cookie is sent regardless of the protocol.
4. Throws an error.

Answer: 2. The cookie is ignored and not sent.
Explanation: Cookies with the `secure` attribute are only sent over HTTPS connections.

What does this code do?

```
document.cookie = "name=Bob; expires=Fri,
31 Dec 9999 23:59:59 GMT";
```

1. Deletes the cookie named name.
2. Sets a cookie named name with no expiration.
3. Sets a cookie named name that expires far in the future.
4. Throws an error.

Answer: 3. Sets a cookie named name that expires far in the future.
Explanation: The `expires` attribute specifies the expiration date of the cookie.

What does the max-age attribute do?

1. Sets the maximum size of the cookie.
2. Specifies the duration (in seconds) the cookie remains valid.
3. Sets the minimum age required for accessing cookies.
4. Clears the cookie immediately.

Answer: 2. Specifies the duration (in seconds) the cookie remains valid.
Explanation: The `max-age` attribute defines the lifespan of the cookie in seconds.

How can you restrict a cookie to a specific domain?

1. By setting the `path` attribute.
2. By setting the `domain` attribute.
3. By setting the `HttpOnly` attribute.
4. By using `localStorage`.

Answer: 2. By setting the `domain` attribute.
Explanation: The `domain` attribute specifies the domain for which the cookie is valid.

What is the effect of setting the HttpOnly attribute on a cookie?

1. The cookie can only be accessed over HTTPS.
2. The cookie is accessible only via HTTP headers and not via JavaScript.
3. The cookie can only be set by the server.
4. The cookie cannot expire.

Answer: 2. The cookie is accessible only via HTTP headers and not via JavaScript.
Explanation: The `HttpOnly` attribute enhances security by preventing JavaScript access to cookies.

Which of the following is true about cookies and localStorage?

1. Both are sent with every HTTP request.
2. Cookies are sent with HTTP requests, but `localStorage` data is not.
3. Both store data indefinitely by default.
4. Both support storing objects natively.

Answer: 2. Cookies are sent with HTTP requests, but `localStorage` data is not.
Explanation: Cookies are included in HTTP requests, whereas `localStorage` data is only accessible via JavaScript.

What happens if you attempt to store a cookie that exceeds the browser's size limit?

1. The cookie is truncated.
2. The cookie is ignored and not stored.
3. The oldest cookie is deleted to make space.
4. Throws an error.

Answer: 2. The cookie is ignored and not stored.
Explanation: Browsers enforce a size limit for cookies (~4KB). If exceeded, the cookie is not stored.

Fetch API in JavaScript

The Fetch API is a modern interface for making HTTP requests in JavaScript. It is built into browsers and provides a simpler and more powerful alternative to the older XMLHttpRequest object.

1. What is the Fetch API?

The Fetch API allows you to:

- Make HTTP requests (GET, POST, PUT, DELETE, etc.).
- Handle responses with Promises.
- Work with JSON, text, blobs, and more as response types.

Example of a Basic Fetch Request:

```
fetch("https://api.example.com/data")
  .then((response) => response.json()) // Parse JSON from the response
  .then((data) => console.log(data)) // Handle the parsed data
  .catch((error) => console.error("Error:", error)); // Handle errors
```

2. Fetch API Features

2.1. Returns a Promise

The `fetch()` method returns a Promise that resolves to the Response object, representing the response to the request.

Example:

```
fetch("https://api.example.com")
   .then((response) =>
console.log(response))
   .catch((error) => console.error("Error:",
error));
```

2.2. Supports Various HTTP Methods

You can specify the HTTP method and additional options using the `init` object.

Example:

```
fetch("https://api.example.com", {
   method: "POST",
   body: JSON.stringify({ name: "Alice" }),
   headers: { "Content-Type":
"application/json" },
})
   .then((response) => response.json())
   .then((data) => console.log(data));
```

2.3. Handles Headers

You can include custom headers in the request.

Example:

```
fetch("https://api.example.com", {
   headers: { Authorization: "Bearer token"
},
})
```

```
.then((response) => response.json())
.then((data) => console.log(data));
```

3. Response Object

The Response object provides methods to work with the response data:

- **response.json()**: Parses the response as JSON.
- **response.text()**: Reads the response as plain text.
- **response.blob()**: Reads the response as a binary large object (blob).
- **response.ok**: Checks if the HTTP status code is in the range 200–299.

Example:

```
fetch("https://api.example.com")
  .then((response) => {
    if (response.ok) {
      return response.json();
    } else {
      throw new Error("Request failed!");
    }
  })
  .then((data) => console.log(data))
  .catch((error) => console.error(error));
```

4. Common Use Cases

4.1. Fetching JSON Data

```
fetch("https://api.example.com/data")
  .then((response) => response.json())
  .then((data) => console.log(data));
```

4.2. Sending Data to a Server

```javascript
fetch("https://api.example.com/data", {
  method: "POST",
  body: JSON.stringify({ key: "value" }),
  headers: { "Content-Type":
"application/json" },
})
  .then((response) => response.json())
  .then((data) => console.log(data));
```

4.3. Handling Errors

```javascript
fetch("https://api.example.com/invalid-
endpoint")
  .then((response) => {
    if (!response.ok) {
      throw new Error(`HTTP Error:
${response.status}`);
    }
    return response.json();
  })
  .catch((error) => console.error("Error:",
error));
```

5. Limitations of Fetch API

1. **No Built-in Timeout**: Fetch does not support timeouts natively.
2. **No Automatic Error for Non-2xx Status Codes**: The .then() block runs even for HTTP errors like 404 or 500. You need to manually check response.ok.

Multiple-Choice Questions

What does the fetch() method return?
1. The response object.
2. A Promise that resolves to the response object.
3. The request object.
4. An HTTP error.

Answer: 2. A Promise that resolves to the response object.
Explanation: `fetch()` returns a Promise, which resolves to a Response object upon success.

Which method of the Response object is used to parse the response as JSON?
1. `response.text()`
2. `response.json()`
3. `response.parse()`
4. `response.data()`

Answer: 2. `response.json()`
Explanation: The `response.json()` method parses the response body as JSON and returns a Promise.

What does this code output if the server returns { "name": "Alice" }?
```
fetch("https://api.example.com/user")
  .then((response) => response.json())
  .then((data) => console.log(data.name));
```
1. `Alice`
2. `undefined`
3. Throws an error
4. `null`

Answer: 1. `Alice`
Explanation: The `response.json()` method parses the JSON, and `data.name` retrieves the name property.

What happens if a network error occurs during a fetch() request?

1. The Promise resolves to an error object.
2. The Promise is rejected.
3. The response.ok property is set to false.
4. Throws a synchronous error.

Answer: 2. The Promise is rejected.
Explanation: Network errors result in the Promise being rejected, triggering the catch block.

Which HTTP method is used by default in a fetch() request?

1. POST
2. PUT
3. GET
4. DELETE

Answer: 3. GET
Explanation: The default HTTP method for fetch() is GET.

What does response.ok indicate?

1. The response is in JSON format.
2. The response status code is in the range 200–299.
3. The response body contains valid data.
4. The response headers are correctly set.

Answer: 2. The response status code is in the range 200–299.
Explanation: The response.ok property is true if the HTTP status code indicates success.

Which of the following can fetch() be used to retrieve?

1. HTML documents
2. JSON data
3. Binary files (e.g., images, PDFs)

4. All of the above

Answer: 4. All of the above
Explanation: The Fetch API can retrieve any type of resource, including HTML, JSON, and binary files.

What does this code output?

```
fetch("https://api.example.com/data", {
method: "POST" })
  .then((response) =>
console.log(response.ok));
```

1. `true` if the request is successful.
2. `false` if the request fails.
3. Depends on the server's response.
4. Throws an error.

Answer: 3. Depends on the server's response.
Explanation: The `response.ok` property reflects whether the server responded with a status code in the range 200–299.

Which of the following headers is commonly set for sending JSON data?

1. `Accept: application/json`
2. `Content-Type: application/json`
3. `Authorization: Bearer token`
4. `Cache-Control: no-cache`

Answer: 2. `Content-Type: application/json`
Explanation: The `Content-Type: application/json` header indicates that the request body contains JSON data.

What happens if the .then() block does not handle an HTTP error (e.g., 404)?

1. The error is ignored.

2. The error is automatically passed to the `catch` block.
3. The `.then()` block still executes.
4. Throws an error.

Answer: 3. The `.then()` block still executes.
Explanation: HTTP errors do not reject the Promise. You must check `response.ok` to handle such errors.

What does this code output if the server responds with a 404 status code?

```
fetch("https://api.example.com/invalid-
endpoint")
  .then((response) =>
console.log(response.ok))
  .catch((error) => console.error("Network
error:", error));
```

1. `true`
2. `false`
3. Throws an error
4. `"Network error: [object Object]"`

Answer: 2. `false`
Explanation: A 404 response does not reject the Promise, but `response.ok` is `false` because the status code is outside the 200–299 range.

What is the purpose of the catch method in a Fetch API chain?
1. Handle successful HTTP responses.
2. Handle network errors or Promise rejections.
3. Parse JSON responses.
4. Automatically retry failed requests.

Answer: 2. Handle network errors or Promise rejections.
Explanation: The `catch` method is used to handle

rejections due to network errors or other issues like invalid URLs.

What does the following code do?

```
fetch("https://api.example.com/data", {
  method: "POST",
  body: JSON.stringify({ key: "value" }),
  headers: { "Content-Type":
"application/json" },
});
```

1. Sends a GET request with JSON data.
2. Sends a POST request with JSON data.
3. Sends a POST request with URL-encoded data.
4. Throws an error.

Answer: 2. Sends a POST request with JSON data.
Explanation: The method is set to POST, and the body contains JSON data with the appropriate Content-Type header.

What does response.text() do?

1. Returns a string representation of the response body.
2. Parses the response as JSON.
3. Converts the response into a binary format.
4. Checks the HTTP status code of the response.

Answer: 1. Returns a string representation of the response body.
Explanation: The response.text() method reads the response body as a plain text string.

Which of the following is true about the Fetch API?

1. It automatically retries failed requests.
2. It supports timeouts by default.
3. It does not reject Promises for HTTP errors like 404.

4. It does not allow setting custom headers.

Answer: 3. It does not reject Promises for HTTP errors like 404.

Explanation: The Fetch API resolves the Promise for HTTP errors like 404 but sets `response.ok` to `false`.

How can you set a timeout for a Fetch request?

1. The Fetch API has a built-in timeout feature.
2. Use a wrapper function with `Promise.race`.
3. Set a `timeout` property in the options object.
4. Use the `fetchTimeout` method.

Answer: 2. Use a wrapper function with `Promise.race`.

Explanation: The Fetch API does not support timeouts directly, but you can implement it using `Promise.race`.

Example:

```
const fetchWithTimeout = (url, options,
timeout = 5000) =>
  Promise.race([
    fetch(url, options),
    new Promise((_, reject) =>
      setTimeout(() => reject(new
Error("Timeout")), timeout)
    ),
  ]);
```

What does the following code do?

```
fetch("https://api.example.com/image")
  .then((response) => response.blob())
  .then((blob) => {
    const url = URL.createObjectURL(blob);
    console.log(url);
  });
```

1. Converts the response into a JSON object.
2. Creates a URL for a binary file like an image.
3. Parses the response as plain text.
4. Fetches and logs the raw binary data.

Answer: 2. Creates a URL for a binary file like an image.
Explanation: The `response.blob()` method reads the response as a binary object, and `URL.createObjectURL()` creates a URL for it.

Which of the following headers is typically required when sending form data using fetch()?
1. `Content-Type: application/json`
2. `Content-Type: application/x-www-form-urlencoded`
3. `Accept: application/json`
4. `Authorization: Bearer token`

Answer: 2. `Content-Type: application/x-www-form-urlencoded`
Explanation: Form data is typically sent with the `Content-Type: application/x-www-form-urlencoded` header.

What happens if you try to access response.json() multiple times?
1. It works as expected.
2. It throws an error.
3. It returns `undefined`.
4. It returns a new Promise each time.

Answer: 2. It throws an error.
Explanation: The body of a Response object can only be consumed once. Accessing `response.json()` multiple times results in an error.

What does the following code output?

```
fetch("https://api.example.com/data")
    .then((response) => response.json())
    .catch((error) => console.error("Network
Error:", error));
```
1. Parses the response body as JSON.
2. Logs "Network Error:" if the URL is invalid.
3. Both 1 and 2.
4. Throws an error.

Answer: 3. Both 1 and 2.
Explanation: The .then() block parses the JSON if the request is successful, and the .catch() block handles network errors.

How can you make a Fetch request with credentials included?
1. Add an Authorization header.
2. Set credentials: "include" in the options object.
3. Use a secure URL (HTTPS).
4. Fetch does not support credentials.

Answer: 2. Set credentials: "include" in the options object.
Explanation: The credentials: "include" option ensures that cookies and credentials are sent with the request.

What does this code do?

```
fetch("https://api.example.com/resource", {
method: "DELETE" });
```
1. Sends a POST request to delete the resource.
2. Sends a GET request to fetch the resource.
3. Sends a DELETE request to remove the resource.
4. Throws an error.

Answer: 3. Sends a DELETE request to remove the resource.
Explanation: The method: "DELETE" option specifies the HTTP DELETE method.

Which of the following is true about handling Fetch responses?
1. Fetch automatically retries failed requests.
2. Fetch treats HTTP status codes above 400 as rejections.
3. Fetch does not handle HTTP status codes as errors.
4. Fetch supports synchronous requests.

Answer: 3. Fetch does not handle HTTP status codes as errors.
Explanation: Fetch resolves the Promise even for HTTP errors like 404 or 500. You must manually check response.ok.

How can you read a JSON response and handle HTTP errors?
1. Use response.json() and check response.ok.
2. Use response.text() for error responses.
3. Use try...catch inside .then().
4. Use response.blob() for JSON.

Answer: 1. Use response.json() and check response.ok.
Explanation: To handle HTTP errors, check response.ok before calling response.json().

What is the correct way to send an API key in a Fetch request?
1. Include it in the query string.
2. Add it to the Authorization header.
3. Store it in a global variable.

4. None of the above.

Answer: 2. Add it to the `Authorization` header.
Explanation: API keys are typically included in the `Authorization` header for secure transmission.

Let me know if you need additional examples or further clarification!

Conclusion

Congratulations on completing this journey through JavaScript! By now, you have built a strong foundation in the language that powers modern web development. You've explored the essentials—from variables and functions to advanced topics like DOM manipulation and error handling—and practiced applying these skills in real-world scenarios.

But this is just the beginning. JavaScript is a constantly evolving language with limitless potential for creativity and innovation. Whether you aim to build dynamic websites, interactive applications, or even venture into backend development, the knowledge you've gained here is your launching pad.

As you move forward:

- **Keep Practicing**: The more you code, the more confident you'll become. Experiment with your own projects, break things, and learn from the process.
- **Stay Curious**: Technology evolves rapidly. Stay updated with new JavaScript features, libraries, and frameworks.
- **Build and Share**: Create projects that solve problems or bring your ideas to life. Share your work with the world and seek feedback to grow.

Remember, every expert was once a beginner. Your dedication and hard work have brought you this far, and with continued practice and persistence, the possibilities are endless.

Thank you for choosing this book to guide your learning. Now, it's time to take your skills and creativity to the next level. Happy coding, and welcome to the exciting world of JavaScript development!

About the Author

Laurence Lars Svekis is a distinguished web developer, sought-after educator, and best-selling author, renowned for his profound contributions to JavaScript development and modern web programming education. With over two decades of experience in web application development, Laurence has established himself as a leading authority in the field, empowering developers worldwide with his clear, insightful, and practical approach to coding.

Laurence specializes in JavaScript, functional programming, asynchronous programming, and front-end web development. His deep technical expertise and passion for teaching allow him to create comprehensive courses and resources that make even the most challenging programming topics accessible. From foundational concepts to advanced features like closures, promises, and async programming, Laurence equips learners with practical skills to build scalable, maintainable, and efficient applications.

With over one million students globally, Laurence's interactive courses, books, and live presentations have become a cornerstone for developers looking to master JavaScript. His hands-on teaching style, enriched with real-world examples, coding exercises, and projects, ensures that learners of all levels gain a strong, practical understanding of the material.

Beyond his role as a prolific author and educator, Laurence actively contributes to the broader web development community. He shares insights, fosters collaboration, and mentors developers, earning him a reputation as a trusted and inspiring voice in JavaScript education. His ability to break down complex technical concepts into simple, actionable steps continues to help aspiring and seasoned developers alike.

Laurence's expertise is especially relevant in today's development landscape, where JavaScript drives frameworks like React, Vue.js, and Angular. His focus on writing efficient, modular code empowers developers to succeed in the fast-paced world of modern software development.

To explore more of Laurence's work, access free resources, and stay updated on his latest projects, visit BaseScripts.com. Laurence's dedication to teaching and community building continues to shape the next generation of developers and inspire innovation in the field.

www.ingramcontent.com/pod-product-compliance
Lightning Source LLC
LaVergne TN
LVHW022300060326
832902LV00020B/3192